getting unstuck

without coming unglued

For ... With best wishes — Susan O'Doherty

A Woman's Guide to Unblocking Creativity

SUSAN O'DOHERTY, PhD

SEAL PRESS

Getting Unstuck Without Coming Unglued
A Woman's Guide to Unblocking Creativity

Copyright © 2007 by Susan O'Doherty

Published by
Seal Press
1400 65th Street, Suite 250
Emeryville, CA 94608

Library of Congress Cataloging-in-Publication Data

O'Doherty, Susan,
Getting unstuck without coming unglued : a woman's guide to unblocking creativity/
Susan O'Doherty.
p. cm.
Includes bibliographical references and index.
ISBN-13: 978-1-58005-206-1 (alk. paper)
ISBN-10: 1-58005-206-1 (alk. paper)
1. Procrastination-Psychological aspects. 2. Inhibition. 3. Writer's block. 4. Work-Psychological aspects. 5. Self-realization. I. Title.

BF637.P76O36 2007
153.3'5-dc22

2007003953

Cover design by Gia Giasullo, studio eg
Interior design by Domini Dragoone

To Bill and Ben:
I love you more than chocolate.

contents

a note on the exercises in this book

e ach chapter of this book includes an exercise designed to help you apply the chapter's main ideas to your own life and goals. If you are like most readers, you will be tempted to skip the exercises. You may think they don't apply to your experience, or maybe you assume you can get everything you need just from reading them. You may even intend to go back and do them at a later time—but that time never comes.

I have certainly read self-help books this way, and I've even benefited from them. You can get a lot from this book just by reading it, too. But often, when I push myself to try the exercises in a book that intrigues me, the experience opens up new, more personal ways of understanding the subject. As the saying goes, we don't get full by reading the menu—and you can't get the full nourishment offered here without picking up a metaphorical fork and digging in.

There are no right or wrong responses to these exercises. I know you've heard this before, and you probably don't believe it. Most artists tend to judge the results of their efforts according to some imagined standard, one that they can never quite meet. Since creativity exercises are by definition open-ended, there is no way to gauge whether our efforts are "good enough," and this can cause feelings of anxiety. So I've included sample responses to give you an idea of the variety of ways clients and workshop participants have used them. I hope they spark your curiosity about how the exercises will affect you and reassure you that they really are tools for self-discovery, not IQ tests.

Sometimes, though, you may try an exercise, but an inner voice will tell you to stop. Listen to this voice. Particularly if you have had traumatic experiences, or if you're not used to self-expression on a deep level, the exercises can unleash powerful emotions. For most women, this is a positive experience: Our responses give us valuable insight into our inner workings and our relationship to our art. But if you find any given exercise frightening or potentially overwhelming, don't tough it out.

Even though I'm a therapist, the advice I give in this book isn't therapy. It can't be, because I don't know you. In therapy, I tend to push my clients past their comfort zones a bit, because I'm experienced at gauging their reactions and I'm able to modify an exercise on the spot based on what they can handle. But since I can't be in the room with you, you need to pay close attention to yourself. If you are puzzled or distressed by something that comes up, I would suggest discussing it with a professional. When you need to explore a disturbing issue, there is no substitute for face-to-face therapy.

Getting the Most Out of the Exercises

Each exercise, like each chapter, builds on the insights of the preceding one. So, to reap the full benefit, it's best to do them in order. If you need to omit one, for the reasons discussed above, that's fine, but try not to skip around—think of the chapters as a course, in which we start with the basics and build up to more complex skills and concepts.

Most of the exercises will ask you to record your responses in the form of drawings, lists, or freewriting. I suggest that you keep these artifacts, in order, in a loose-leaf binder (see Materials You Will Need, below). Taken together, they will constitute your artistic autobiography, building a picture of important episodes in your past, issues that affect your current relationship to your art, and possible directions for future work. You can go back to the entries and add to them as new insights occur to you, and you can review them when you feel stuck and in need of inspiration or encouragement. Some participants even use their artistic autobiographies as the raw material for stories, conceptual art, and autobiographical performance pieces.

Materials You Will Need

- A loose-leaf binder
- Writing paper (small enough to fit into the binder)
- Drawing paper (small enough to fit into the binder)
- A hole punch, if the writing or drawing paper doesn't come with prepunched holes
- Pens, colored pencils, crayons, and any other drawing material you enjoy using
- Loose-leaf dividers, one for each exercise, labeled with the title of the exercise

A Private Place

To get the most out of these exercises, you will need a block of uninterrupted time (usually about a half hour for each exercise) and a private space to enable you to concentrate on them. It's often hard for women to claim time and space for ourselves, especially if we have young children. But for an artist, these are necessities, not luxuries.

You don't need an entire room of your own, though of course that's ideal. A small table in a corner, which your family or room-mates know is off-limits, is fine. Even a packing box that you can keep under the bed when you're not using it will do in a pinch. What's important is that you keep the materials for your artistic autobiography together and accessible when you need them, and that it's clear to the people around you that they are yours alone, not communal art supplies or an interesting project that they can snoop in.

While doing the exercises, you will need privacy. If your family is able to leave you alone in the bedroom while they watch TV in the living room, that's great. If not, you'll have to get creative. You may be able to trade off childcare with a friend, or to convince your spouse or partner to take the kids to the zoo for an afternoon. Or you may need to set up shop in a quiet corner of the library or a coffee shop, constructing your own private space in the midst of strangers. This can be awkward if you have an emotional response to any of the material, but then again, you wouldn't be the first person to burst into tears at Starbucks. One client brings her writing and drawing material to the bus station, because, she says, no one pays attention to anyone else there.

Doing the exercises "right," assembling the perfect materials, or ensuring total privacy are not what's important. To make the exercises work for you, what is paramount is approaching them with an open mind and an attitude of honest exploration. Dive into them; have fun with them; surprise yourself. And please do let me know how they work for you—visit my website, www.susanodohertyauthor.com, and leave me a note. I look forward to hearing from you!

author's note

elizabeth, Lisette, Janna, Bonnie, and Maria are the "stars" of this book. Their stories will illustrate the ideas and principles I discuss in each of the chapters. They are not actual people—they are composites of clients, friends, and women who have attended my workshops—but the issues they struggle with are real, as are the discoveries and practices that have helped them to develop as artists and as human beings. I will also introduce the voices of real artists who have agreed to share their thoughts and experiences to help others who are struggling.

why i
wrote
this book

Introduction

this letter came to me in care of my weekly online advice column for writers, "The Doctor Is In."

Dear Dr. Sue,

I've lost my writer's voice. I know what happened to it—when I was a beginning, energetic writer, I fell in with a very destructive critique group who told me that everything I was interested in writing was wrong for the genre I was writing in. And I listened because this group included three published authors and one nominee for a major award. In my enthusiasm, I obeyed every rule they pounded into me. I cut the wealth of description, the depth of character emotions, my natural usage of various points of view. My writing is a poster child for why most editors nay-say critique groups: It's homogenized to the point of being bland. I realized this several years ago and have been trying to recapture something of what I was (I have the manuscripts from that time, so I can see what I used to do and how much more real it is than what I produce now), but have had no success.

I've tried freewriting, but I can't do it. Day after

day, I'd sit there with pen and paper, ready to write whatever came to mind, but my mind was blank. Literally. Fifteen minutes of absolutely no thought. Day after day for a month of staring at a blank page. A friend of mine says that I've got massive filters built onto my creativity, so it's almost impossible for me to turn them off. Probably true, since when I try to do anything new and different, I get that "blank mind" from trying to spark ideas. When I tried the morning pages that work so well for many friends of mine, I got the same "blank mind" state. I'm told that I have to allow myself to get silly, but I can't. I don't know how to "get silly," I guess.

When I query agents I get requests to see my material, but in the end I'm always rejected, and I think my lack of "voice" is the reason.

Any suggestions on how to shut off or deconstruct these blasted filters? Shy of seeing a professional (I'm unemployed, but searching), I'm willing to try pretty much anything.

—*Silenced*

Dear *Silenced*,

I think your friend is probably right about the creativity filters, but I doubt that that is the whole problem. I wonder whether, in addition to feeling stifled by this group, you may be mildly depressed. This is just a guess—I don't know anything about you beyond the information in your letter—but I am imagining the following scenario:

You, a vibrant and enthusiastic beginning writer, join a writing group whose members are more accomplished than you and have impressive credentials. They inform you that the parts of your writing that are most personal to you—that are most expressive of your unique personality—are worthless and must be excised.

At roughly the same time (again, I'm guessing), something goes wrong at work. You are laid off; the company moves to another state and you decline to move with it; you quit for another job that doesn't materialize. You search for a new position, but nothing quite works out.

You continue to query, and you are met with respect and some interest, but in the end your work is rejected, repeatedly.

Do you detect a theme here?

There isn't one, really. Writers tend to identify patterns and connect random events, to find—or create—meaning in a chaotic universe. We also take negative criticism as gospel while letting praise roll off our backs. A series of events that are tenuously connected, at best, filtered through a writer's sensibility, might make it seem as though the universe is sending you the message that you don't have what it takes to be a writer. In reality, you stumbled into a viper's nest, you are suffering a vocational setback, and you are getting some attention for work that you acknowledge is not your best. But I imagine that, in Jim Croce's words, that's not the way it feels.

Try letting yourself off the hook for a while. Don't force yourself to write. Read whatever interests you, without regard to whether it will improve your writing. Watch mindless TV. Spend time with friends who care about you and will support you whether or not you ever write another word. In other words, don't force anything.

Chances are good that you will find a new job. As your finances and sense of security grow, you may find yourself once again feeling playful and resilient. Ideas for new work, or new approaches to your existing books, will pop into your head while you are drinking your morning coffee, or commuting to work, or cooking dinner. Write these ideas down without putting pressure on yourself to make anything more out of them before you're ready. But if you feel like elaborating a bit—again, without any goal other than to play with an interesting idea—do that as well.

It's likely that you will be able to ease yourself back into writing, in your original, sparkly style. If, after the rest of your life is back in order, your writing continues to feel bland or blank, you may wish to speak to a professional to explore the reasons for this group's continued hold on you.

In my practice, and in the workshops I give on overcoming creative blocks, I often see intelligent, creative women, like Silenced, who have lost touch with the inner voice that directs them to produce their best work. Some had childhood dreams of becoming an artist that they didn't pursue because they never developed faith in their gifts. Others painted, wrote, or composed enthusiastically until they hit a roadblock—a devastating rejection, a loved one's disapproval, or simply the cultural message that women—especially those with children—have no business taking time away from their families to indulge in making art (or competing in a male arena).

And yet, these dreams don't die. They express themselves indirectly, in vague dissatisfaction with everyday life; in an extra glass of wine or helping of chocolate cake to push down that feeling of dull despair; or in envy, jealousy, or avoidance of those who have "made it"—particularly other women.

I can help these women because I used to be one of them.

From the time I learned to read, I dreamed of writing books that would shape and transform my readers' worlds as my favorite books did mine. I wrote my first book at age five—an illustrated tome about a beautiful princess and her pet dachshund. As a "brainy" girl growing up in the 1950s and 1960s, though, I was often cautioned by well-meaning adults to "play dumb" so as not to alienate boys. Young ladies were good listeners, cheerful companions, and loving nurturers. Loud, opinionated bookworms were left sitting alone at the dance. College, at least in my family, was for boys; girls went to secretarial school, and, if they played their cards right, married the boss. I was eager to be liked, so I did my best to appear cute and nonthreatening, with some success.

It was a bargain with the devil, though. What I gained in popularity, I lost in autonomy and self-confidence. In my efforts to understand and support the views of the boys I was interested in, I lost track of my own dreams and interests.

I'm far from alone in this. In my practice and my workshops, I see many women who, despite their intelligence and accomplishments, routinely play down their advantages to present themselves as attractive and nonthreatening. When this repudiation of our gifts becomes a habit, too often we forget we're pretending. We start believing that we are less talented and competent than we really are, that we are less entitled to our opinions, that we are not serious and don't deserve to be taken seriously. We may know, deep inside, that we are brilliant, creative, and strong, but when we continually hide and deny this, and the culture supports our denial, the pretense begins to feel like reality.

I was eleven in 1963 when Betty Friedan published *The Feminine Mystique,* kicking off the second wave of feminism. Even so, the idea that women were equal to men took a long time to trickle down to my suburban town. (Some would say it hasn't gotten there yet.) My mother, and many of my friends' mothers, opined loudly that Friedan and "all those women's libbers" were just angry and bitter because men didn't find them attractive.

We got the message. Girls were supposed to concentrate on being pretty and desirable, and the bar for that was very high. In 1966, when I was fourteen, the impossibly skinny, leggy fashion model Twiggy was named "The Face of '66" by the influential *London Daily Express*. Suddenly miniskirts were *de rigueur,* and fashion magazines were spouting inspirational slogans such as "Thin is *in!*" My friends and I—healthy, normal-looking teenagers—counted calories obsessively, dividing food groups into "good" (lettuce, celery, diet soda, and little else) and "evil" (bread, potatoes, and chocolate). Some of my friends started swiping their mothers' diet pills.

Strict rules governed hairstyles. Hair was supposed to be stick straight, regardless of one's ethnicity—except that it had to curl up or under at the ends, either in a "flip" or a "pageboy." So we spent hours rolling or ironing our hair and then slathering it with styling gel to "tame those ugly split ends." Eye makeup, including heavy mascara and sometimes even false lashes to emulate Twiggy's wide-eyed look, could take an hour to apply—and this was just to go to school. There was barely time or energy to devote to reading, writing, or making art.

Even after 1968, when the "youth revolution" was supposed to liberate us from the constraints of fashion, the pressure didn't let up; it just went underground. We were supposed to pull off looking sexy and chic in faded blue jeans and peasant shirts while serving homemade brownies to the men who were doing important political organizing. Fashion magazines gave us tips on bleaching our jeans to the perfect romantically faded hue and on tie-dyeing our own blouses.

All of this emphasis on our looks—and we always fell short of the fashion magazine ideal, no matter how hard we tried—reinforced our beliefs that appearance was what mattered most about us, and that we weren't good enough as we were. And every accommodation I made to fashion and popularity took me another step away from the self-confidence that would have allowed me to express myself through writing.

In my honors English classes we read Hemingway, D. H. Lawrence, and James Joyce. I loved Joyce's verve and admired Lawrence's intensity and Hemingway's spare and elegant style, but I longed for stories that explored the nature of friendships, love relationships, and the social order from a woman's point of view. I found such books on my own—novels such as Jane Austen's *Sense and Sensibility* and *Persuasion*, in which intelligent and thoughtful women struggle to balance the demands of family and society against their own romantic inclinations; George Eliot's *The Mill on the Floss*, about a headstrong and passionate young woman whose insistence on acting morally, rather than correctly, leads to her destruction; and Charlotte Brontë's *Jane Eyre* and *Villette*, stories of two impoverished and plain women who find purpose and dignity in self-reliance and hard work. My teachers considered these "minor classics" at best and steered me toward more "important" writers. Women, it seemed, were suitable as material and inspiration for writers, but men were the designated creators.

So I grew up knowing that I was as smart as the boys and at the same time doubting it. Other women have reported this dual consciousness—the feeling that we know things that we aren't supposed to know, or that would be dangerous to say. Some come to therapy and confess that they think they're "crazy." And, of course, if you think that expressing your deep knowledge will brand you as "crazy," you're going to do your best to stay on the surface—which does not make for the creation of great art.

I knew I was bright, because I did well on tests and I was good at writing papers, as long as they didn't demand that I choose a controversial position and defend it. In class discussions, though, the boys dominated. They would state their opinions about world affairs or Joyce's place in the literary canon with such authority! Even when they were challenged, they didn't seem to get confused or back down. I could sometimes see holes in their arguments, but when I tried to articulate them, I became tongue-tied, afraid that I only *thought* I understood the issues because I wasn't smart enough to know what they were really talking about. My friends may have felt the same way, but I don't know because we never talked about this. I wish we had.

Times have changed since then. Teachers are more enlightened about gender issues, and the definition of "great" art has opened up a bit. Still, when I worked as a therapist at an inner-city elementary school in the late 1990s, teachers used to punish boys who misbehaved by making them walk in the girls' line when the class traveled from one place to another, and high school students report that although girls are now recognized as capable scholars, conventional scholarship itself is often denigrated as boring, uncool "girl stuff." The action—and money—are in technological fields where girls are often made to feel unwelcome. And young women continue to worry that they are crazy for questioning the idea that our society functions purely as a meritocracy.

I entered college in 1970, the first year my school—previously the women's college of the University of Virginia—began admitting men. Women still made up most of the student body, and teachers made an effort to include writing by women in our literature courses. So I discovered Virginia Woolf, Simone de Beauvoir, and Zora Neale Hurston—writers who challenged and refuted the assumption that women, and women's concerns, were "minor." By that time, though, it was too late. I no longer trusted my voice. Like Silenced, I had become convinced that the ideas and feelings that sprang from my deepest self—the qualities that made my writing unique—were the ones that had to be tossed. My writing was cautious and flat, because I was more focused on avoiding stupid mistakes than I was on expressing my ideas.

So I turned to acting in college and kept it up when I moved to New York after graduation, marshaling my empathy and intelligence to interpret the ideas of (mostly male) playwrights and using my own creativity in the service of theirs. In New York, I worked—first as a proofreader for a law firm (where I met my husband), then as an editor of romance magazines—while I auditioned, took acting classes, and, occasionally, acted in plays at night. I went on to write speeches for the president of New York University and then to head the development writing staff for the campaign to restore the Statue of Liberty and Ellis Island. I liked reading other women's stories, and I had a flair for selecting and editing them—the two magazines I worked on grew dramatically more popular during my tenure. I enjoyed the challenge of devising persuasive and eloquent speeches and program descriptions. I loved using my imagination to inhabit dramatic characters and bring them to life. Yet all of this work entailed subjugating my skills to the representation of others' ideas.

I did write poems, short stories, and even a one-act play on the side. Some of my poems and one story were published, and my play was produced. But I knew something was missing. My work was facile and clever, but except for the play (which I wrote in a frenzy, almost as if I were trying to outrun my internal censor), my writing only occasionally touched on my real beliefs and concerns. At that point, I didn't really even know what those were.

When I acknowledged, in my early thirties, that I needed to plan for a long-term, reliable career, I chose to return to school to become a drama therapist. I had studied acting with some brilliant teachers, and I found that the improvisational exercises we performed not only enhanced my acting technique, but they illuminated aspects of my psyche in ways I hadn't understood before. When I was given the task of acting out an argument with a woman playing my mother, for example, I would hear myself saying things to her that surprised me. Later, when the class would discuss the scene, other actors would share their impressions of the interaction. I nearly always came away with valuable new self-knowledge. I was excited by the idea that I could use these techniques to help others explore and address their issues.

I turned out to love the work of therapy. I loved helping my clients tell their stories through improvisation and other dramatic techniques, and I loved working with them to create new and better endings, first for the dramas they enacted and then in their lives. I became fascinated by the components of the creative process, especially the question of whether it is possible to nurture creativity in people who don't seem to have natural artistic ability, and I wrote my master's thesis on the development of creativity in children with Down syndrome. After a few years, I decided that therapy that focused on developing creative ability was my life's work. I returned to school yet again to become a clinical psychologist.

Not until 1991 did I seriously question any of these decisions. That year, having finished all of my psychology course work and having embarked on my clinical internship, I became blocked in writing my doctoral dissertation. My thesis was that writing autobiographical fiction could address and heal developmental wounds through imaginatively reworking important events and relationships. I intended to illustrate my argument with examples from the life and work of Christopher Isherwood, whose novel writing had apparently helped him transform himself from a repressed and hostile upper-class snob into an emotionally generous and fulfilled artist.

Isherwood was born in 1904 into a wealthy, upper-class British family. He absorbed the cultural messages of his time and social class, including racism and class snobbery. When he was eleven, his father was killed in World War I. Isherwood apparently suffered a complicated bereavement reaction, which expressed itself in extreme anger at his mother. This anger lasted into his adulthood, dominating their interactions and interfering with his other relationships. His early writing is brittle, superficial, and saturated with rage and contempt, especially for characters who are mothers or mother figures.

A complex interaction of personality and environmental factors, including his homosexuality, failing out of Cambridge and then out of medical school, and moving to Berlin, where he observed the rise of Nazism, caused Isherwood to question the environment he was raised in. He began writing detailed, relentlessly honest diaries, exploring his psyche and relationships, which he transformed into autobiographical fiction. As he did so, his attitudes toward himself, his society, and, especially, family relationships grew more flexible, accepting, and inclusive. He was able to integrate these changes into his life, embracing Vedantism and apprenticing himself to a Bengali guru (a revolutionary act for a member of a white colonialist family); finding and nurturing a mutually fulfilling love relationship that lasted until his death; and, perhaps most dramatically, reconciling with his mother. Writing was not the only cause of these changes, of course, but his memoirs and novels make clear that he used his imagination to work out conflicts through the medium of fiction, deepening his understanding of his own motives and the possible motives of friends, strangers, and antagonists, and achieving self-knowledge and acceptance of others that informed and enhanced his "real" life. I was fascinated by this process and determined to learn as much as I could about how it worked.

I absorbed, even inhaled, the novels, biographies, and psychological literature on creativity and emotional development that served as the background material for my study. I thought and talked about it constantly. But I couldn't write a word.

I consulted three therapists who helped me explore the possibility of fear of success, fear of transcending my family's gender expectations, fear of not being good enough. None of it sat right. I was nervous about these things, but I had achieved success in other areas in which I was not supposed to excel— after all, I had edited two popular magazines, written speeches for the president of a major university, and served as the chief development writer for two of the country's most visible and important landmarks—and I knew I was at least as competent as other therapists at my level of training.

When it finally occurred to me to consider the content of my dissertation, I realized that what was holding me back was grief—grief for my dream of being a writer myself, for the possibility of a life devoted to self-expression—for my lost voice.

So I decided to use my study of the creative process not only to help others but to help myself. As I read Isherwood's work again, one fact jumped out at me: As a privileged male, he felt entitled to write about and publish his most intimate, self-exploratory thoughts and experiences. He assumed that others would find his inner processes as fascinating as he did. (And they are fascinating. His work is not just narcissistic rumination; it is accomplished art. But it starts with the assumption that his life held intrinsic interest—an assumption that I, and many women, did not share about our own lives.)

Up until the moment of that discovery, I had assumed that the reason Isherwood had written important novels and memoirs and I had not was that he was a real writer and I was a hack. This changed everything.

In the first place, just identifying the issue freed enough energy so that I was able to write my dissertation. After graduation, I began to explore the impact of gender on creativity and artistic expression. I revisited the courageous women writers of the past, such as Woolf and Beauvoir, who had found the courage to speak over the patriarchal proscriptions of their times. I immersed myself in the work of feminist psychologists such as Phyllis Chesler and philosophers such as Adrienne Rich. I practiced, slowly and painfully, writing what I really thought and felt rather than what I thought others wanted to read. I began writing stories and essays that reflected my experience—stories about women who struggle with self-esteem, relationships, and family issues. And, somewhat to my surprise, my stories were accepted by literary journals and anthologies.

In 1999, after working for others for all of my adult life, I opened my own psychotherapy practice. It started as a general practice, but after I helped a few writers overcome creative blocks, they sent their friends and colleagues to see me, and soon writers and other artists made up the majority of my clients. Most of them are women.

I love working with artists. I love the process itself—delving into a client's past experiences and current situation to help her discover both the source of her blocks and the strength and wonder of her gifts. I find it deeply satisfying to walk into a bookstore and see a wonderful book written by someone who didn't believe she could write and to know that I helped her achieve her dream.

I feel privileged to do the work I do. But my ability to help others doesn't mean that I've resolved all of my own issues. I continue to struggle with self-confidence, with feeling entitled to spend time and energy on my writing, and with believing that anyone else will find my work interesting or worthwhile. Even now, as I manage my psychotherapy practice and write this book, I find myself apologizing to my husband and son for our less-than-immaculate apartment and quick, unimaginative meals—as though housekeeping were my sole responsibility and a much more important function than my professional work. The men in my life are not my oppressors—they pull their weight and support me wholeheartedly, and they couldn't care less about dust bunnies and canned soup—but my early training is still with me, and I need to confront and overcome some aspect of it every day. I do this by reminding myself daily that I have a right to pursue my dreams. I set aside one day a week in which I do nothing but write for eight hours—I don't do paperwork, I don't pick up the dry cleaning—I don't even answer the phone. As much as it goes against the grain, I have learned to say no to requests from friends, relatives, and even the PTA if they interfere with my sacred writing day. I do freewriting exercises to overcome my fear that my writing is boring or stupid. And I use everything I've learned, and continue to learn, to help my clients confront and overcome their own obstacles.

In this book, I will give you a peek into my practice and into my own life story. I'll share tools to unlock and nurture your own creativity, including exercises that will help you make sense of seemingly mysterious phenomena such as procrastination on a project you love, fear of success, and friends' and loved ones' lack of support at crucial times. We've all been through times when we stared at a blank computer screen in despair because the words wouldn't come no matter how intensely we willed them, or when we avoided the corner of the den where that half-finished painting seemed to mock us. But as we come to understand the forces, both internal and external, that inhibit us from acknowledging and expressing our deepest selves, we can also develop the tools to nurture our expressive powers. By sharing my own journey and the journeys of other creative women, I hope to encourage and motivate you to begin that novel, finish that painting, or identify and pursue a dream you may have buried so deeply it feels forgotten.

what we learned at home

Chapter One

trying to create art while weighted down by negative messages is like driving with the emergency brake on—it's possible to get where we want to go, but it takes much more energy, we don't have nearly as much fun, and we can damage our vehicle. We may never completely rid ourselves of the assumptions and self-doubts we were raised with, but as we bring them to conscious awareness and examine them, they become more manageable, and our work becomes deeper and richer.

When a new client comes to see me, the first thing I do is take a complete history. I ask about the issue that has spurred this initial visit and what moved her to come in now, as opposed to, say, six weeks, or six years, ago. We talk about her current life situation, and then we move backward in time to her childhood experiences so that I can get a sense of how the problem may have started and other ways it may have manifested in her life.

When women consult me about feeling stuck in their creative work, I often start by asking them to try to remember the messages they got as children—and particularly as young girls. Often these messages conflict with both their innate sense of themselves and their real world experiences. For example, Elizabeth first consulted me because she no longer felt motivated to write. Her novels—thoughtful, sensitive explorations of relationships among family members, friends, and lovers—have a small but loyal and literate following, but she had never been able to take her work completely seriously. Now, at eighty-two, she had begun to take stock of her life, and she felt she had wasted much of it writing silly and frivolous books. Although she was in excellent health, she recognized that she had limited time left, and she wanted to either fulfill her true artistic potential or give up writing entirely.

Elizabeth had learned from her blue-collar, no-nonsense family that life consists of hard, grinding work, and that, in her words, "a woman's place was in the home, serving her husband and raising the children. Any striving for beauty or accomplishment was squelched as 'silly' or, worse, 'putting on airs.'"

Elizabeth's father, a mail carrier, was an alcoholic who became angry and violent when he drank. Her mother worked as a waitress in the evenings, and when she was at home she was exhausted and impatient. Her brothers were constantly fighting, except when they ganged up to throw Elizabeth into the creek behind the family's home, to break into her piggy bank, or to behead her dolls.

When Elizabeth was in the fourth grade, her class took a field trip to the town's public library. "It was a Carnegie library," she told me, "one of those elaborate Victorian edifices built by the industrialist to bring culture to the masses. To my nine-year-old eyes, it was a castle. It had huge chandeliers, walnut paneling, and ornamental plasterwork. The children's room was bright and spacious—and quiet. It was everything my home wasn't."

Elizabeth started spending all of her free time in the library and befriended the children's librarian, who recommended books to the dreamy little girl. "One day she handed me *Little Women*," Elizabeth said, "and transformed my life. I was entranced by this story of four girls who struggled with hardship and loss and yet strived to make their lives loving, beautiful, and meaningful."

Elizabeth decided early on that she wanted to be a novelist. "Actually, I would have chosen to be a character in *Little Women*, if I could have. Amy, probably—I was in love with Laurie, and I wanted to live in that big, luxurious house. But since I couldn't do that, the next best thing was to create my own stories, my own worlds. When I was writing a story, I was able to inhabit its world even more fully than when I was reading. It was when I felt most alive, most myself."

Elizabeth began writing stories and submitting them to women's magazines. She had her first acceptance when she was fourteen. "It was a story about a wealthy couple whose marriage was deteriorating. Obviously, I had never heard the saying, 'Write what you know.'" Other acceptances followed.

"My parents were glad for the money, though they couldn't understand why anyone would pay me for 'that nonsense.' My father told me I was very clever to have come up with a way to make money without working. They didn't understand at all, and I couldn't explain it to them.

"Even so, I was proud of myself, and in school I started giving myself airs about being an 'authoress.' I would even argue with my teachers—something that really wasn't done back then, especially by a girl—because I felt I had greater authority, being a published author and all. I must have been insufferable.

"Finally, Mr. Halloway, my eleventh-grade English teacher, who considered himself a scholar, took me aside one day after class and told me what he thought—what he said all serious intellectuals thought—of 'ladies' magazines.' I guess I had it coming. He told me that if I were to become a real writer—which he wasn't sure I could do, since I was a girl and interested only in frivolities—I needed to study the 'classics'—Shakespeare, the Greeks, Chaucer, and Milton, mainly, and then some of the newer important writers—Sinclair Lewis, D. H. Lawrence, and Hemingway. They were 'real' writers, not dilettantes.

"I certainly needed to be taken down a peg, and his advice, to study classic writers, was good. I followed it religiously, reading my way through Shakespeare first, and then onward in time according to a reading list he prepared for me. Then we would talk about the books, and often he would give me writing assignments based on what I had read. It was tremendously helpful, and I know that the discipline and exposure made me a much better writer.

"The problem was, I came away with the idea that all of the important writers were men, and all the books worth reading had to do with politics, power, war, and murder." Not only that, but her teacher's instructions played right into the message Elizabeth had gotten from her family, that a preoccupation with beauty or feelings was girlish, stupid, and a waste of time.

After high school, Elizabeth went to work as a salesgirl at a women's clothing store in town. She spent every spare moment writing stories and working on a novel, trying to incorporate the lessons of the classic works she continued to study. She published her novel at twenty-one. "It was a mess—a sorry mélange of all of the 'great books' I had devoured but not really digested yet. It was about the devastation of a French city during the Occupation, but I had never been to Europe and my understanding of politics was fairly rudimentary, just what I read in the papers, like everyone else. I was trying so hard to be 'important' that I forgot to include believable characters or plotlines." The book garnered unenthusiastic reviews and dismal sales, "as it should have." Elizabeth, deflated, decided she wasn't really a novelist after all.

Like many women, Elizabeth had fallen into a trap: Convinced that her own experiences and perceptions were not important or interesting, she tried to emulate the work of artists she admired and had been taught were superior. But because her writing didn't express her own, unique worldview, it lacked the spark and originality that separates art from hack work. Typically, Elizabeth blamed herself and thought that her novel's failure was confirmation that she was untalented.

Two months after her book's unhappy publication, she fell in love with Richard, a handsome Air Force pilot just home from the war. They were married within the year. "I tried to re-create the worlds of my beloved girls' books in real life," Elizabeth said. "I spent all my energy creating a beautiful home, baking delicious cookies, volunteering for the PTA, being a Girl Scout leader, trying to make life beautiful and serene for my family. When my husband was home, I wanted everything to be perfect for him. Did I miss the life I'd plotted out for myself, the quiet library, the important books, publication, tea with writers I admired? Of course I did—but most of the time I was too exhausted to realize it."

The cultural environment of the '50s didn't support "career women," especially those who were married with children. And Elizabeth had received powerful messages from her family about a woman's place. She had the resources to keep house on a more luxurious and aesthetically pleasing level than her own mother had, and this was a source of conflict for her—her family felt uncomfortable in her home and resented her for "putting on airs." Still, she was conforming to their basic dictum that she should devote herself to "serving her husband and raising the children."

If she had lived in a different era or had come from a more supportive background, Elizabeth might have recovered from her novel's failure and tried again, but she didn't see that as an option. It wasn't until she was in her mid-forties, when her husband divorced her to marry a young flight attendant, that Elizabeth started writing again—and her motivation this time wasn't artistic excellence or fame, but desperation. "I felt lost," she said. "Canceled out. And, for the first time, I really started questioning the messages I'd grown up with, that marriage and family were the only acceptable sources of fulfillment for a woman. My children were grown; my husband had decamped; and all that was left was a beautiful, empty house and the empty shell of what used to be a vibrant, hopeful young woman. Writing was the only way I knew to find my way back to myself.

"I had been burned with my novel, and I didn't think I'd ever try 'serious' literature again. But I had had success with those stories for women's magazines. I had subscribed to all the major ones throughout my marriage and, frankly, the magazines hadn't changed very much from 1938 to 1968. I decided to give it a go."

Her first effort met with immediate success. "Ironically, it was a reworking of my original story about the well-to-do couple with an unraveling marriage," she said. "But now I was writing from experience. And those years of studying the 'masters' did pay off. I understood much better now how to structure a story and the importance of the telling detail."

Painful circumstances had forced Elizabeth to recognize that her family's model for female behavior was not valid for her. She loved her husband and children, but pouring all of her energy into meeting their needs had kept her from identifying and address-ing her own, so that she was left feeling "lost," "canceled out," and "empty" when they didn't need her anymore. Unlike many women, she had experienced some early success, and this helped her real-ize that there were other roads to happiness besides the one her family and society endorsed. Even though Elizabeth did not yet take herself seriously as a writer, she had at least dropped her efforts to imitate the "important" literature that she was not equipped to write and had begun to express her own feelings and thoughts.

Simply unearthing these deeply ingrained messages about what our families and society expect of us drains away some of their power, as we see them for what they are—not proclamations from on high, but the often mistaken assessments of people who saw us, and the world, through the distorted lenses of the belief systems of their own families. And once we discover that these were messages from long ago that don't truly reflect the truth of our goals or abilities, we can begin to move forward.

I had to review my own family's history and transmitted messages after I became blocked in writing my doctoral dissertation on the healing power of fiction writing. Once I acknowledged that what was stopping me was my own thwarted desire to write fiction, I needed to look back and figure out how I'd come to believe that I was not smart, talented, or original enough to write.

□ □ □

When I was in elementary school, I became hooked on a series of girls' books that described the adventures of a plucky young nurse named Cherry Ames. I didn't actually want to be a nurse— even then, it was clear that biology and chemistry weren't going to be my strong points—but I was entranced with the life-and-death hospital drama, the friendships among the nurses, and her serial romances with handsome young doctors. I shared my enthusiasm with my grandmother, who confided that when she was growing up at the turn of the century, she had dreamed of becoming a nurse. I thought she would have made a fine nurse—

better, even, than Cherry Ames. She was a supremely competent household manager who managed to make running a clean, orderly home and cooking elaborate meals seem effortless; she was capable of moving the furniture around herself if she was in a decorating frenzy and there was nobody home to help her; she wasn't grossed out by dirty diapers or vomit the way I was; and she wasn't intimidated by anyone. She corresponded with heiresses and princesses she met on her travels abroad, and she once, famously, gave a piece of her mind to a policeman who had stopped my grandfather for a traffic infraction. (The officer told my grandfather, "I was about to give you a ticket, but I see you've got enough trouble.") She could have handled any of Cherry's dilemmas with strength and aplomb.

In 1914, when World War I broke out in Europe, she was sixteen and had never left her hometown of Petersburg, Virginia, but she was ready to travel overseas and sign up. Her father forbade it. According to him, girls from "good families" didn't touch men they weren't related or married to, and they didn't clean up "other people's messes." She met my grandfather the following year and married him in 1922, after he returned from the war. Instead of saving lives and pursuing adventures, she dedicated her life to making a home for her husband and, later, her two children. She continued to exert her strong will, but in less direct ways— engineering her children's social lives, terrorizing domestic workers and yard staff, and, after his retirement, convincing my sedentary grandfather that he really wanted to travel the world.

My mother also had her dreams. A straight-A student, she hoped to attend college to become a teacher. My grandparents weren't opposed to this in principle, but college was expensive, and my grandparents disdained scholarships as "charity." They thought that it was more important to send her brother to college because "he will be supporting a family," whereas my mother would just get married and have children. That was what middle-class women in the 1940s were expected to do. The rare woman who pursued a career was either pitied (as unmarriageable or, if she was married, as pathetic because her husband couldn't support her) or whispered about as a lesbian, because homosexuality was thought to be a mental illness back then.

So my mother became a secretary and got married—she met my father when she worked in his office. She loved her job. She was, and is, highly organized, efficient, and sociable, just the person you would want running your office. But she left her job when I was born and stayed home until my younger brother was in high school.

"Stayed home" isn't exactly accurate—she channeled her prodigious energy into serving in various official capacities for our local Women's Club, serving on the Board of Directors of the town's Visiting Nurse Association, and volunteering for such thankless positions as Brownie leader and Cub Scout den mother. She didn't hold a paying job, but I seldom saw her with her feet up, either.

I hadn't been aware of any unhappiness or frustration on her part with being a homemaker all those years, and she certainly never complained about her life, but when she returned to work—not because she wanted to, of course, as she was quick to assure us, but to help out with college tuition—it was as though she had been returned to herself. She would come home in the evenings bubbling over with stories about her boss and coworkers. She sometimes apologized for the franks-and-beans or frozen lasagna she threw together at the last moment. My brother and I didn't know how to tell her that we enjoyed these improvised dinners more than the ones we had to praise to the sky because she had slaved over them. Those elaborate feasts may have tasted better, but these were much more fun and interesting.

□ □ □

My mother and her mother were the two most powerful female influences in my childhood. You might think that two intelligent and resourceful women whose own ambitions had been quashed would have made sure I was spared the same fate—but of course life doesn't work that way. When we push down our anger about our own unfair treatment—because we love our families and want to believe they are acting for the best—this shapes the way we look at ourselves, the world, and our children. So although both my mother and my grandmother were forthcoming about the dreams of their youth, both also framed their stories with statements about how "silly" and "unrealistic" and even "selfish" their ambitions had been, and how they were much happier and better off in their rightful places, at home with the children.

rother was perfectly smart, but he was dys-
g this comparison about as much as I did.)
r was shocked when I told her, at twenty-
ing married. She had never believed I would
And she expressed gratitude and relief that
Jewish, because "Jews know how to take care
don't expect them to work."
also transmitted to me many of the cultural
e. She taught me that men run the world, and
t belong in positions of power because we don't
issues well enough. And the kicker: that ugly
angry because men don't find them attractive. My
teer experiences—especially organizing and lead-
unruly and often rambunctious Brownies and Cub
ld probably have qualified her to run a major cor-
a small country, but she insisted that these activities
g" and that men did the real work.
ther, one of nine children of Irish immigrant parents,
thusiastic reader and lover of literature and art in gen-
e believed that the *creation* of art was the province of
group, certainly no one from our family. The messages
m my father had to do with not getting above my (his)
If I had aspired to become an accountant, like him, or
broker, he might have been moved to support me, even
I was a girl. But a writer? Clearly, I needed to be pulled off
gh horse.

I took in a number of messages from both my grandmother and my mother, many of which were reinforced by the culture at large. I learned from them, as Elizabeth learned from her family, that a woman's place is at home, caring for her husband and children, meeting their needs rather than addressing her own. Both claimed to be totally fulfilled by homemaking, as did nearly all of the women I saw on TV. I grew up watching *Leave It to Beaver, Father Knows Best,* and *The Donna Reed Show,* three popular TV programs that featured husbands who went off to work and elegant, articulate wives who seemed to be perfectly happy to stay home, cooking, cleaning, and raising the children. The only "career woman" I remember seeing on TV, outside of two servants (Hazel and Beulah on their respective shows), was Sally on *The Dick Van Dyke Show.* The premise of the show was that Rob (Dick Van Dyke) was the chief writer for a television comedy show. He supervised two talented comedy writers, Buddy and Sally. Their jobs seemed fascinating to me—they brainstormed creative comedy routines for the show's star and engaged in witty repartee (at least, it seemed witty to a ten-year-old) among themselves. By contrast, Rob's pretty wife, Laura, seemed to lead a boring and monotonous existence caring for their young son in the suburbs. Yet everyone on the show felt sorry for Sally because she wasn't married, and Sally herself announced frequently that she would gladly trade her job for a husband—an unlikely event, since she was not conventionally pretty and had an aggressive personality. Probably the most popular show of that era was *I Love Lucy,* in which Lucille Ball's efforts to achieve autonomy and an identity separate from her husband were routinely shown to be ridiculous and doomed to failure.

When the culture at large reflects and reinforces the messages we get from our families, these messages begin to feel like universal truths. If what we want is different from what everyone says we're supposed to want, we tend to question what's wrong with us, diverting time and energy that could be used to prepare for and pursue our dreams.

My grandmother was focused on appearance as the way to win a "good" husband (i.e., one with the means and motivation to support and spoil his wife). She had done well for herself this way. She was from an old Southern family that had lost all of its money in the Civil War. Her family was upset by her alliance with the son of an Irish immigrant tavern keeper, but my grandfather, who stayed enamored of my grandmother through more than fifty years of marriage, became an accountant and made very wise stock market investments. My grandparents achieved a higher standard of living than either of their families had ever known.

In return, my grandmother, in addition to her homemaking, made it her business to be immaculately dressed and groomed, even for a day at home or a trip to the supermarket. She thought that my grandfather deserved a beautiful wife to go with his beautiful home. She also believed that an attractive wife was an asset to her husband's career, and she took pride in cultivating and entertaining my grandfather's business associates and their

wives
father

My
I seemed
about how
tiveness did
nail polish, sh
father would v
would be to tak
Avenue for "real" c
and I would raid tł
your grandfather wor
When I was ten, she re
Chanel suit for me. Sh
had not cut her beautiful,
it instead in coronet braid
took me to them for stylish

The results never matc
straight enough to please her.
hair, ruining the results of the s
how lacked "sparkle." I "always ha
my voice when I was upset or excit
quently and vocally, saying what a
and personality went to the boy while
(In fact, she and I looked very much ali
was stunning, so that's how people expe

you're wondering, my b
lexic. He loved hearin
My grandmothe
three, that I was get
"catch" a husband.
Bill, my fiancé, was
of their wives. The
My mother
beliefs of her tir
that women don
understand the
women are all
mother's volu
ing troops of
Scouts—wou
poration or
were "nothi
My fa
was an en
eral, but
an elite
I got fro
station
a stoc
thoug
my h

It took me many years just to recognize that my dreams of writing were not just childish nonsense, and it took even longer to identify the ways I had been deeply influenced by ideas I didn't agree with. Many clients in my practice are also held back by beliefs passed down from their families and reinforced by the culture. One of those was Lisette.

□ □ □

Lisette, a forty-six-year-old African American composer, was raised with the double bind of gender expectations and race. She grew up in an upwardly mobile, primarily African American suburb of Atlanta in the 1960s and 1970s. Lisette's father, Dan, was a commercial architect. He eventually achieved success, but when Lisette and her brother, Adam, were young, Dan had trouble finding steady work because many white business owners were hesitant to hire him. When money was tight, Dan supplemented his income by designing and building wooden furniture. Even in the leanest times, there was never any question of Lisette's mother, Lavinia, going out to work.

"It was a very loving home, a musical home. I adore my family. But the messages I got were strong ones: Men go out in the world, develop skills, accomplish things. Women stay home and look nice and take care of everyone. And my father's difficulty made it clear to me that a black professional, no matter how talented and hardworking, is going to have a hard time."

Lisette's brother, Adam, took piano lessons in their home

from the age of eight. Six-year-old Lisette would creep into the living room during his lessons, drinking in every detail. She practiced Adam's lessons when no one was around. She learned to read music, to place her hands correctly on the keys, and the basics of timing. She composed her first song at the age of seven. "It was definitely the work of a seven-year-old kid. I was no Mozart. But I had taught myself the rudiments of musical notation and written a song all by myself, for both hands. I was so proud!"

Lisette was discovering her vocation. But when she played her song for her parents, they laughed at how "cute" she was, and when she asked them for lessons of her own, they told her that the family couldn't afford them. "They said they had enough money for Adam's piano lessons and my ballet lessons, and that was that. But I didn't want ballet lessons. I was short and squat and had no talent at all, so I was stuck in a class that was just little suburban girls bouncing around in pink tutus and everyone smiling at how adorable we were. I hated the whole experience. I wanted to create music, not dance to it. But they wouldn't let me quit."

Families and cultures differ in their assessments of what constitutes "important" work. According to most of my female clients, though, there is one constant: The activities that are most valued tend to be assigned to the males. Lisette's family considered music important. They were active in their church, where music played a large part. Lisette's mother sang in the primarily female choir; the organist and choir master were men. Composing, directing, and playing music were considered male activities; singing, though a challenging and demanding discipline, was discounted as "natural," because even children could sing without formal lessons. Social and economic forces came into play, too: "Both sides of the family were descended from slaves," Lisette said. "Nearly all of my great-grandparents were sharecroppers and field hands, and both of my grandmothers cleaned other people's houses. For my mother to be able to stay home, and for me to do something so purely decorative as ballet—there was obviously no way I was training to be a dancer or dance teacher—meant that they had made it securely into the middle class. But back then I felt they were telling me that no matter how hard I worked, I would never be good enough to deserve what fell right into Adam's lap."

From the age of seven, when she wrote her first song, Lisette knew she wanted to be a composer, but she never told anyone. "My family would have laughed and patted me on the head, and I couldn't bear it. Besides, I didn't think there were any women composers. How could I plan for a career I didn't know existed?"

Like Elizabeth, and like me, Lisette learned from her family and culture that her own talents and inclinations were less important than the roles she was expected to play because of her gender. Lisette's father's experience also colored her expectations of what she would be allowed to achieve in the mainstream, white world. Often these early lessons become deeply embedded in our psyches and are difficult to uproot; they start to feel as if they are a part of us.

Lisette pushed her dream underground. She didn't give it

up—she continued to compose through her high school years, but in secret. She didn't believe her work would ever be performed, and she felt sheepish and almost shameful continuing to write music. "I felt I was doing something wrong, unnatural," she said. She tried to focus on becoming a music teacher instead. Her parents approved of this ambition, at least as a stopgap until she married and had children. "At least it was a way to stay connected to music," she told me.

Lisette entered a small northeastern women's college in 1978. She made few friends, and again she didn't confide her dream to anyone. "It was kind of a snobby place—a little out of our social and economic range, what my parents wanted for me. It wasn't exactly racist, but the other women were friendly and standoffish at the same time. They were nice to me because nobody wanted to be the kind of person who was rude to a black girl, but they didn't try to get to know me, either—not that I helped much with that. I'd gotten used to hiding the most important part of myself, and I guess that made me pretty boring to be around.

"I also wasn't learning much that interested me. The education department at my school was strong, but the music department was only so-so. By that time I was aware of a few female composers, but the music department wasn't really into composition, and anyway, I was a music education major, not a 'real' musician. All in all, I felt isolated." Lisette virtually stopped writing music in college because "it seemed hopeless. It was never going to happen. I decided I needed to grow up and get real."

Then, at the beginning of her junior year, everything changed. Her college had a visiting-professor-in-residence program, and that year, the visiting professor was a distinguished composer, and a woman.

"At first, I avoided her," Lisette said. "I felt I had already given up my dream, and being around her would just open old wounds. Besides, she was from an old-money WASP family, and I decided that she would be snobby and competitive. I hated her without ever talking to her. I was jealous, of course, and scared, but I didn't know that at the time. I was only twenty, and a young twenty, at that.

"Then, second semester, I took a music notation course with her. I pretty much had to do it; I needed the credits and hers was the only class that fit the rest of my schedule. I dreaded it. But she was a wonderful teacher, enthusiastic and patient."

Lisette had spent much of her life so far developing "protective pessimism"—trying, out of fear of failure or ridicule, not to hope for what she wanted most. It was easier for Lisette to believe that the two strikes against her in the eyes of mainstream culture—being black and female—meant certain failure. It was safer not to try than to make herself vulnerable to her family's censure and the contempt of the white world.

Protective pessimism can be an adaptive response. Opening ourselves up repeatedly to rejection or ridicule is damaging, and Lisette's experiences so far had not given her reason to believe that she, a black woman, could be taken seriously or supported as an artist. But we pay a price when we settle for safety. If we never risk failure or disappointment, we can never know if we might have achieved our dreams.

Lisette's experience with Christine, her professor, frightened her because it challenged her protective pessimism. Lisette's first, understandable impulse was to stay hidden, not to rock the boat. But an inner voice of strength and health prevailed. She marshaled her courage and took a risk.

"One night at a department party, I had several glasses of wine. That helped me get up my nerve and ask if I could play her some of my compositions. We made an appointment to meet in one of the rehearsal studios the following day.

"I was nervous and tight, but she was encouraging. She gave me very helpful criticism. She didn't laugh at me or belittle my ambition. She took me seriously. On the way back to my dorm afterward, I broke down and cried. After all those years of not admitting, even to myself, how much I wanted this, I knew that my future was set. I was going to be a composer. There would be no going back."

Today, Lisette teaches in the music department of a major university. Her compositions have been performed by orchestras around the world. Her brother, Adam, who is now a partner in their father's architectural firm, remains a gifted amateur.

It might seem that Lisette had "won"—she achieved success in her chosen field despite all the forces working against her. But she entered therapy because she was blocked, not in her work, but in her life. Adam had a wife and children, and he basked in the approval of his family and community. Lisette, by contrast, had few friends, had never been in love, and felt like an outsider wherever she went. Her early experience of being forced into the mold of "good little girl," and the need to defy the expectations of her family and culture to pursue her music, had left lasting scars. She felt unable to share her deepest self with others. She was afraid that a lover would pressure her to change, to become more conventionally feminine, and that if children entered the picture, she would be expected to give up her music entirely. "I don't want to live this way," she told me. "Adam never had to choose between being taken seriously and being loved. I don't regret my choice, if there has to be a choice—my music is who I am. But if there's another way for me, I want to find it before it's too late."

For those of us, like Lisette, who have had to fight for our autonomy, it can feel as though the world is just waiting for us to show a chink in our armor, to drag us back down to what it considers our proper place. And when we've been taught that men are strong and ambitious and women are soft and compliant, we often feel compelled to reject our "feminine" side—the part of us that is open to relationships and to love—if we are to succeed in the world. So we withdraw from others, pretending we don't care, because we are frightened of how much we do care—how vulnerable we feel ourselves to be, how intensely we long to be on the inside of a charmed circle instead of always standing on the outside, watching. We fear that giving in to our desire for ordinary human relationships will make us weak and that we will lose everything we fought so hard for.

With Lisette and other clients who channel their sensitivity and love into their art while presenting an indifferent or even hostile face to the world, the work focuses on helping them realize that they are entitled to define themselves and to set their own boundaries. As a child, Lisette was controlled by the beliefs and preconceptions of the adults around her. As an adult, she had choices—she could reject relationships with people who tried to change or undermine her and pursue those that supported her. But first it was necessary to identify and address those preconceptions and their impact on her developing self.

□ □ □

Janna also struggled with issues of vulnerability and self-definition in a very dramatic way.

Sometimes young girls have to deal with more than just harmful messages from their families and culture. I also see women struggling with the devastating, long-lasting effects of sexual, physical, or emotional abuse. Artistic expression can help trauma victims to process their rage and grief. Some gifted women, like Janna, take this therapy even further and use their experiences to fuel the creation of remarkable works of art. The ability to transform pain into art is impressive but not necessarily a sign that healing is complete, as Janna related to me when she first started therapy.

Janna is a twenty-six-year-old painter who grew up in a small Midwestern town. Both of her parents were physicians who encouraged Janna and her younger sister, Elaine, to believe they could accomplish anything they were willing to work at. As a child, Janna didn't plan to be an artist. She excelled at science and was good with her hands; she assumed she would become a neurosurgeon like her mother.

Janna's parents divorced when she was six and Elaine was four. Her father, a cardiologist, moved to another house in the same neighborhood. Because both parents' schedules were busy and unpredictable, a live-in nanny had always cared for the girls. Fay, their nanny, now shuttled between houses with them. Their parents worked hard to keep the girls on an even keel. "It wasn't that tragic," Janna told me. "We were sad that we weren't all living together, but we weren't crippled by it or anything. If that was the worst of it, I'd be finishing medical school now."

Janna's father remarried. Her new stepmother, Carla, was "nice enough. She wasn't my mother, but she didn't have to be— my mother was three blocks away."

Then, when Janna was eight, her mother met Louis. "He was trouble," Janna said. "Elaine and I both knew it. At first he was too nice to us—he brought us expensive toys, and if we said anything remotely funny, he'd laugh his head off. We weren't having it, but when we tried to tell my mom what bad news he was, she thought we were just jealous. She kept reassuring us that there was no need to feel threatened, that we would always be a family and 'her girls' would always come first."

Janna continued:

Then they got married, and his first move was to fire Fay, our nanny. This was more traumatic than my parents' divorce. Fay had been with us since I was born!

Louis convinced my mother that since he ran a video distribution business from home, he could look after us just fine. Fay was an unnecessary expense and got in the way of our "bonding" with him. Elaine and I fought it, but Louis was very persuasive.

The short version is, the "video distribution business" was a front for a child pornography ring. I won't go into the things he made us do in front of the video camera. He told us he'd hurt our mother if we "tattled" on him. He also convinced us that no one would believe us—that just doing these things showed that we were bad little girls, and if we told, everyone would watch us naked on their TVs and make fun of us.

I was nine then, and Elaine was seven. She started getting into fights at school. I just shut down—I stopped eating, stopped doing my school-work, stopped talking to anyone. Our parents and teachers thought it was a delayed reaction to the divorce and remarriages, all the disruption. They put us in counseling, but guess who was the one to bring us to our appointments and do most of the talking to the counselor, because he was around? It was a complete farce.

This went on for more than a year. Then, in the fourth grade, we had an assembly where a psychologist talked to us about sexual abuse. She told us about how abusers say things that aren't true to keep the victims from telling. I realized that was what Louis had been doing.

I went up afterward and talked to her. She came with me to tell the guidance counselor, and he called child protective services and my mother. Louis was arrested. Later, he went to trial, and Elaine and I both testified. He's in prison now, forever, I hope.

Our whole family—Elaine and me, my parents, and Carla—went into therapy together, for real this time. It helped a lot. What helped me most was the therapist's suggestion that since I had such a hard time talking about my feelings, I might try making art from them. I started painting and writing poems. There were huge parts of myself—joy, playfulness, and healthy anger—that I thought were lost forever, but through art I found them again. I never showed my work to anyone, though, not even to Elaine. For school assignments, I wrote "nice" poems, of the "roses are red" sort, and painted pictures of kittens with little hearts over their heads. I kept my real work stuffed in my underwear drawer at Mom's house, which the family was forbidden to open on pain of death.

I don't blame my mother for what happened. I'm sure if we'd been able to tell her, she would have protected us. But I was still angry at her for not noticing, for being away so much and not believing us when we said Louis was a creep.

It all erupted when I hit adolescence. She couldn't do anything right as far as I was concerned. She already felt guilty about what happened, and I got pleasure from rubbing salt in the wound.

One day we got into an argument about something stupid—whether my skirt was or wasn't too short, I think—and it all came spewing out in a poem. I wrote in a frenzy—about Louis, about how much I hated her for not protecting me, about how she had given up the right to rule my life, and then, as I calmed down, about how much I loved her. I left it on her pillow. Afterward, I got scared. I thought maybe she'd be enraged or terribly hurt. I went to get it back, but she'd already read it. And, fortunately, she got it. We both cried, and talked for a long, long time, and we've been close ever since.

Heartened by her mother's response, and feeling hopeful that her artwork really could communicate the thoughts and feelings she couldn't say aloud, Janna submitted her poem to the literary magazine at her high school—and her mother was called into the guidance counselor's office. "He thought my mother would be shocked to read what I had said about her," Janna said. "But she and I both knew that it was really about a 'nice girl' writing such angry poetry." The poem was rejected by the journal, and Janna was encouraged to submit one of her "nice" poems. She refused. With her mother's support, she started submitting this poem, and others like it, to small literary journals, and within a year, two of her poems were published.

"They weren't great poems. My medium is visual art, not words. But I think the editor responded to them because they were raw and real, passionate. This acceptance, and my mother's support, helped me to address the next big issue I was facing— my sexual orientation.

"I'd felt for a long time that I was a lesbian, that I had strong feelings for girls. I liked boys and had crushes on a few, but my real passion was for girls. I'd kept that, like everything else, under wraps for a long time, but once I started communicating through my artwork, it was hard to stop."

Janna told the family's therapist about her feelings. The therapist urged her to confide in her mother. "Mom blamed herself at first. She felt that what Louis did had turned me off men. It wasn't anything like that. The feelings had started before Louis was even in the picture, though I couldn't have articulated them. Besides, I'm crazy about my dad, and my sister is as straight as they come. This is me, who I am. Once my mother could see that, she was okay with it, with me. It took my dad a little longer, but he came around, too. The therapist helped a lot."

Janna was fortunate to have such enlightened parents and a skilled therapist who helped her accept herself as a strong, intelligent woman, as an artist, and now as a lesbian. But there was a huge difference between their attitudes and those she encountered at school. When she entered an erotic painting of two women embracing in the annual art show, which had open submissions, the art teacher, the administrators, and some of her fellow students objected to its inclusion, claiming it was "inappropriate." ("It was the poem all over again. My mom was grilled by the guidance counselor, and I was urged to submit a landscape. We stuck to our guns, and this time we won.")

The unwavering support of her parents, especially her mother, allowed Janna to continue to develop her creativity and individuality in the face of opposition. She believed what her parents had taught her—that she could succeed at anything she devoted herself to. But she felt like a misfit at school, where the teachers distrusted her and most of the other students gave her a wide berth. "Who knows, I might have been like them, if I hadn't gone through so much," she said. "I might have been a cheerleader, and made pretty art, and repressed my sexuality to fit in. I might have been happy that way. But that's not how my life worked out. I was angry and rebellious, and except for a few other oddballs, I didn't have friends."

Janna moved to New York shortly after she graduated from high school. She got a job as a word processor for a large law firm, moved into a small apartment in a marginal outer-borough neighborhood with roommates she found on an Internet bulletin board, and enrolled in art classes at night. Her teachers were impressed and supportive, and she began exhibiting her work when she was nineteen. Her paintings have attracted notice for their often violent and disturbing imagery. "I try to turn my childhood feelings of fear and victimization on their head," she explains. She paints pictures of children that portray them as both sexualized objects and individuals in pain. Some galleries won't touch her work; others court her for what she feels are the wrong reasons: "Some guys get turned on by my stuff. That's not my intention—or, rather, my intention is to make us question why it might be a turn-on, to look inside ourselves."

Last year, a parents' group tried to have one of her paintings—a preadolescent girl stepping out of the shower, looking aghast, as though she realizes that she can be seen—removed from a local show on the grounds that it was "pornographic."

"It's the opposite of pornographic," Janna argues. "In pornography, the women are portrayed as having no individuality, no shame. They don't resist. Their one desire is to please men, whatever that takes. That lets the abusers off the hook—they can pretend that the victims are asking for the abuse, that they want it. In my pieces, the women are being used, but they have feelings about it. It's the feelings that compel me."

The attempt to remove Janna's work from the show drew attention from local media. She is articulate about the source and intention of her work, and the coverage was generally supportive. The picture stayed in. Even so, Janna felt shaken by the experience. "It was like high school all over again. There were all these people calling me names and saying my work isn't art, it's sick and kids shouldn't be exposed to it. What about the real things that happen to kids?

"I should be used to this by now, to being hated for expressing what I see as the truth. It was a nightmare, though, and I realized there was still a lot I hadn't dealt with." That was when she came to see me.

The messages Janna received from her immediate family and the family therapist were caring and supportive. These helped her to survive a horrendous experience and to transform her pain and rage into art. The pain and rage were still there, though, and continued to haunt Janna. So did the lack of support and understanding she had experienced in her school community. Janna needed to revisit her childhood and adolescence and put some old ghosts to rest before she could move on. This was where our work began.

□ □ □

Janna's parents gave her many advantages. This is admirable, but it's important to remember that they were able to do this because they were privileged in certain ways—economically, educationally, and socially. Other parents may want to support their children, but they are overwhelmed by poverty, emotional and physical exhaustion, and a lack of educational resources. This was Bonnie's situation.

Bonnie is a forty-two-year-old photographer who initially entered therapy because of a crisis in her romantic relationship that was affecting her work. (I'll discuss this crisis in detail in Chapter Six.) We went over her early history to identify themes that could give us insight into her current unhappiness. This is what she told me:

She is the third of five children from a poor family in the mountains of Appalachia. "The TV programs used to refer to our county as a 'depressed area,'" Bonnie recalled. "I thought they meant the people. I suppose it all went together. Our area was built as a company town for a coal mining company. I was four years old when the company pulled out. All the jobs disappeared." Bonnie's father moved to a nearby city in search of a new job, "but soon he disappeared, too."

Bonnie's mother worked as a supermarket cashier—the only job she could find—but she did not make enough to feed and clothe the children. The family went on welfare. "A series of men moved in—I guess my mother thought they would save us," Bonnie said. "They would help with the bills for a while, but then they would move on, or they'd lose their jobs and lie on the couch all day, drinking, and then Momma would kick them out, and we'd be back where we started.

"Everyone I went to school with talked about leaving town," she said. "On the one hand, we knew there was no future for us if we stayed, except for odd jobs, welfare, drinking, and kids. On the other, though, we couldn't imagine any other life. We'd watch TV shows about glamorous people living in big cities, and it was as if they were from another planet. My sister wanted to be a famous singer—but she got pregnant at fifteen, and that was that." Her sister's boyfriend called her a "slut" and refused to marry her, and, according to Bonnie, "abortion was just not a word we knew." Bonnie reported that her sister, now married to another man, is happy with her life, but said, "I would have killed myself if it had happened to me. Yet I didn't think there was anything else out there for me, either."

To make the right choices for ourselves, we must first be aware that we have a choice. Bonnie, her siblings, and her class-mates felt disconnected from the larger culture. They may have dreamed of becoming singers or television stars, but they knew there was no realistic way to accomplish this or many other potential goals.

In addition to talent and motivation, an artist needs guid-ance and training. Most very poor people don't have access to these advantages. Although Bonnie liked looking at pictures, she never went to a museum or took an art class. Those were not options in her town.

Then, when she was twelve, a large photographic film com-pany sponsored a photography-in-the-schools program, and

Bonnie's middle school was chosen to be part of it. The company supplied inexpensive cameras and film to all the students, with instructions to shoot whatever interested them. "Most of the kids took it as a big joke—they took pictures of each other's behinds, or they made faces in the mirror—you know, kid stuff. Some of the girls got all dressed up and took formal pictures.

"It was different for me. When I put the viewfinder to my eye, I immediately saw the world differently. I was fascinated by an inchworm crawling up a tree, the way it curved itself to move forward. I suddenly noticed how old and tired my momma looked, how beautiful my sister was, and how the light filtered through our dusty kitchen window and played on the dishwater. I took pictures of it all. I cried when the film ran out—I knew I'd never get another chance like this."

Bonnie hadn't realized that the cameras were only the beginning. The children's photographs were developed and displayed in the school, but they were also sent to a panel of photographers and critics, who selected one child from each region to participate in a fully funded summer arts program in Boston. To Bonnie's joy and amazement, she was chosen.

The summer program was an ordeal in many ways. The children stayed in a college dormitory, loosely supervised by their adult teachers. Bullying was common, and most of the teachers either didn't notice or didn't care. The other students made fun of Bonnie's crooked teeth, shabby clothes, and what they called her hillbilly speech. They assumed her selection had been a fluke. But there was no denying the magic that transpired when Bonnie looked into a camera.

One of her teachers, Frank, a well-known photographer, took Bonnie under his wing. "He had incredible patience," she said. "I was a real pain and determined not to waste a minute. He answered all my questions, lent me books, and critiqued my pictures. I got better and better. That made the other kids hate me even more, though. They spread rumors that I was giving Frank blow jobs and that's why he paid so much attention to me. It was torture."

Despite the social land mines, this was a life-changing experience for Bonnie. "For the others, it was another credit to put on their college applications. For me, it was the window to a new life. I was determined to pursue photography when I was old enough to move to a city and get a job. That seemed very far off, though, and I knew all too well that anything could happen between now and then. They let us keep our cameras—good ones, this time—but I knew we couldn't afford film or developing. When I packed my camera, I wondered how many years it would be before I got to use it again."

So she was stunned to find a package waiting for her at home. It was from her mentor, Frank, and it contained rolls of film and prepaid mailing envelopes addressed to him. All year, she took pictures and sent the film to Frank. He would develop them and send her two prints of each—one plain print, and one covered with comments and criticism. "So I kept learning," Bonnie said.

Bonnie spent the following summer, and every summer until she graduated from high school, living with Frank's family in New York City and working in his studio. "Another family might have felt there was something strange about this arrangement," Bonnie said. "They might have wondered if this older man from a big city was interested in their daughter for the wrong reasons. They might have insisted on meeting him. For my family, it was one less mouth to feed, one less child to worry about, thank the Lord."

After her high school graduation, Bonnie moved to New York. With Frank's help, she found an apartment and a job at a magazine, archiving photographs and occasionally submitting one of her own for publication. From there, she began getting freelance assignments at that magazine and others, and she eventually became a staff photographer for a news magazine.

"I've seen the world," Bonnie told me. "I make good money—enough so my momma and my sister and brothers don't have to worry about paying the bills. It's been a fight every step of the way—against the people who thought I was a stupid hillbilly who wasn't worth bothering with, and then, later, against the men who thought a woman shouldn't be taking pictures in a war zone or a militarized area. But this is my life. Taking pictures is who I am—and nobody is going to take that away from me, ever."

The primary messages Bonnie took in from her early experiences were that nothing would be handed to her and that she was lucky for any advantage that came her way—and she needed to struggle and fight to keep it. She viewed the series of events that set her on her career path—first the photography contest, and then Frank's interest—as strokes of great luck, which they were. Bonnie was certainly not the only bright and promising child in her community, and she never forgot that if the photographic company had chosen a different school or a less sympathetic teacher, she might well have ended up like her sister, an impoverished single mother at sixteen with her options closed off. It's good that she remains aware and appreciative of her advantages, and that she continues to help her family. But the gratitude and industriousness engendered by her early experiences have a dark side.

Bonnie felt that she was on her own in a world that was indifferent at best and often hostile and treacherous. Her family and community were too overwhelmed to support her. Her father's disappearance, followed by her mother's transient relationships and then the defection of her sister's boyfriend, left Bonnie feeling that men were unreliable and would leave women to feed and care for their families through grinding work and personal sacrifice. The first peers she met outside of her community were brutal and competitive, and afterward she had a hard time believing in her peers' goodwill. Perhaps most damaging of all, Bonnie didn't give herself credit for the talent and determination to take advantage of her luck, and she was never able to completely relax and enjoy the success that she had earned. She divided people into "friends" (anyone who was recognizably kind to her) and "enemies" (those who behaved in a way she interpreted as unfriendly, even if the "unfriendliness" was based in shyness or reserve or was a reaction to something Bonnie herself said or did). She was slavishly devoted to her "friends" because she didn't think she deserved the attention of educated and interesting people—and some people sensed this and took advantage of her. Even with those who genuinely cared for her, such as Frank and, later, Bonnie's boyfriend, Steve, Bonnie felt too insecure to make personal demands or set limits on what they could ask of her. She felt honored by their interest and would do anything to keep it. When Steve's wishes or demands conflicted with Bonnie's best interests, she found herself sabotaging her career—which is how she came to start therapy. As for her "enemies," she was too frightened and distrustful to engage with them, either to work out differences or to fight back. She just kept her head down and concentrated feverishly on her work and on pleasing the people she cared for. Worst of all, she was terrified that all of her good fortune could be snatched away from her as quickly—and, seemingly, randomly—as it had come.

□ □ □

Bonnie felt she had narrowly escaped a stultifying life taking care of children. Maria, with a greater range of choices, was thrilled to be a mother. But parenthood intensified her deep-seated insecurity about her self-worth and the worth of her art. The seeds of this insecurity were planted and took root during her childhood.

Maria is a twenty-eight-year-old poet and short story writer of Puerto Rican descent. She was born and raised in the Bronx, where she still lives.

Maria grew up in a warm and loving extended family. Her father was the superintendent of the apartment building where Maria lived with her parents, her grandmother, her older brother and sister, and her younger brother. Cousins also lived in the building, a secure haven in a dangerous and drug-infested area. Maria never lacked playmates or loving supervision. "Even so," she said, "I always felt different—not better or worse, I just didn't fit in, even though I looked like everyone else in my family, wore the same clothes, and talked the same mixture of Spanish and English. The things I thought about were different, and the *way* I thought was different."

As a young child, Maria fell in love with the power of words. "I was always pestering my family to read to me and to tell me stories," Maria said. "I loved stories, especially the silly or fantastic ones. I loved it that things could happen in books that you never saw in real life—that Cinderella's pumpkin became a coach, that bears could talk, that Charlotte could save Wilbur from being slaughtered by writing in her web. This was my world, the one I wanted to live in."

When Maria was four, her older sister, Cecilia, taught her to read. Eight-year-old Cecilia loved playing schoolteacher. "We would have 'lessons' every day when she came home. We'd go over my favorite books, the ones I knew by heart, and she'd make me sound out the words."

Maria vividly recalls the moment she learned to read. "I was staring at the word 'airplane' and saying it, over and over, and suddenly I was *reading* it. I had cracked the code! From that day on, there was no stopping me."

Fortunately for Maria, nobody tried to stop her—at least, not then. Both of her parents had dropped out of school to help support their families. They thought their lack of education had held them back from many job opportunities and social advantages, and they were determined that their children would be better equipped. "If anything, they were even more supportive of the girls," Maria said. "Both of my brothers were very active, a little too active, my parents felt. My older brother, Ernesto, was interested only in sports and music, and the baby, Manny, was always in trouble. I think now he was hyperactive, but back then they just labeled him a 'bad kid.' So Cecilia and I were the ones who were encouraged to work hard, to study, and to get ahead. My parents pushed to get us into programs for gifted children, and they went without to make sure we had the proper books and supplies."

The encouragement came at a price, though. "For my family, education meant obeying the rules—learning what the books said, becoming an 'expert.' Their idea of a smart, educated person was a doctor, a lawyer—somebody in a structured profession who made a lot of money, brought honor to the family, and could build them a big house back in Puerto Rico.

"Cecilia was good at that, at doing what was expected. She

still is. She's an accountant, married to an accountant. They have a nice house in New Jersey and three beautiful, smart kids. They give money to my parents. Everyone is so proud of her. I am, too. But I'm not like that. I could never play by the rules."

In elementary school, Maria's vivid imagination and precocious verbal skills earned her high marks, pleasing her family. Later on, though, the subjects she excelled in—art, creative writing, and drama—were eliminated or downplayed in the curriculum, and by the end of middle school she had fallen behind in the "important" subjects—math, science, and history. Success in those areas demanded organization, memorization, and attention to detail, skills Maria struggled to master.

"My paintings and stories meant nothing to my parents and teachers. They thought I was playing around, like a little kid in a sandbox. They kept telling me I was going to have to grow up and get serious. But math, science, and even history and geography bored me, at least the way they were taught in my school, and I stank at them. I was just no good with numbers and formulas, or the dates of battles or the gross national product. They didn't mean anything to me. So my grades tanked. In fact, I started thinking that everybody had been wrong about me, and that I was really stupid—that I'd just managed to fool them for a while, and now it was all falling apart. Once I decided I was dumb, I stopped trying. I just daydreamed in class and wrote poems instead of taking notes. Eventually I had to drop out of the gifted program and go to a neighborhood school, with tougher kids. Then I just sat in the back of the classroom and tried to be invisible—I never wanted to draw attention to myself.

"Those feelings have never really left me. I still feel stupid and incompetent, like the things I'm good at aren't worth anything. And I hate to be put on the spot or to be the focus of attention."

Science, math, and social studies can be enormously creative pursuits. They are certainly important disciplines that can lead to fulfilling careers. The basics can be hard for an imaginative child with a restless mind to master, though, especially as they are taught in many schools—by rote memorization without a connection to context. Some talented girls are subtly (and not so subtly) discouraged from excelling in more technical fields because of gender bias, but I don't think that was Maria's issue. Her interests and abilities lay elsewhere, on the more artistic side of the spectrum—the side that is often devalued because it is not "practical" and rarely leads to conventional success, and because, in some cultures, it is associated with softness and femininity.

Like Elizabeth, Maria absorbed the message that the activities she loved and that reflected her deepest thoughts and feelings were second-rate. In Elizabeth's case, it was specifically women's writing that was considered "frivolous." In Maria's family, artistic activity itself was valued lower than skills that were likely to lead to a steady paycheck. But in both cases, the result was self-doubt.

Cecilia, a straight-A student, won a scholarship to a large university with a prestigious business school. Ernesto went to college on a baseball scholarship. But no scholarships were forthcoming for Maria. Instead, she lived at home while attending a local community college, where she did well in literature and barely passed the required math and science. She then transferred to a four-year school in the city college system. Though Maria didn't know it at the time she applied, this school had a strong creative writing program. It was there that the tide turned for her. "The people I met were like me—dreamers, misfits, people who colored outside the lines. It was like finding another family, one that saw and understood me," she said.

Maria began writing stories about life in the Bronx. Some were realistic, others fantastic and dreamlike. Her teachers encouraged her to submit them for publication. When she got her first acceptance, she ran to tell her mother. But she didn't get the response she wanted. "She wanted to know how much they would pay me. It was a literary journal—it paid in copies. She thought I was stupid to waste all that time on something that didn't pay. I was twenty-one years old, she said, and still playing little-girl games." Even worse, when the story came out, her family was angry. "It was about a girl whose brother gets hooked on drugs," she said. "Manny was having some problems then, but the story wasn't about him. They couldn't understand that. They felt I had brought shame on the family—and not just the family, but the neighborhood, and the entire Puerto Rican community. They said, 'Everyone will think that's all we do—sit on the stoop and drink beer and take drugs.'"

Maria felt miserable. She wanted to please her family and gain their approval, but this seemed impossible without turning into a different person. With the encouragement of her teachers and fellow students, she continued to write her stories and poems and to submit them to journals. More acceptances followed, but she didn't mention these to her family. Instead, she shared her good news with her creative writing community at school. Through some of her classmates, she became active in a vibrant circle of writers and artists who identify as both New Yorkers and Puerto Ricans, popularly known as "Nuyoricans."

Maria met her husband, Jim, in a fiction writing class. "He was really a pre-law student, but he dabbled in writing," Maria said. "He was quite talented, I thought. But, like my parents, he considered writing to be a hobby and law to be a real, adult profession." They dated off and on for several years. After graduation, Jim went through law school and Maria worked in a bookstore while she honed her writing skills. Gradually, Maria's stories were accepted by some of the more important journals, and her work became known, especially among the Nuyorican group—"a real thorn in my grandmother's side," she said wryly.

As her work became better known, another problem surfaced. Since her public-school days, Maria had avoided drawing attention to herself for fear of exposing what she considered her "stupidity." Now she was asked to perform at readings. "I make myself do it," she said, "because it's part of being published. You have to get out and let people know who you are—at least, that's what everyone says. But I hate it. I always throw up first, and then I'm afraid the sound of my knees knocking together will drown out my voice. I imagine the audience thinking, 'Who the hell does she think she is, wasting our time with this crap?' I think that when I submit to journals, too, but at least the editors can't see me."

Meanwhile, living at home was increasingly difficult. Her family was offended by Maria's writing and disappointed in her seeming lack of ambition. Her father couldn't understand why a college graduate would take a clerical job in a bookstore, and he experienced Maria's job and writing as personal affronts. At one point things got so tense that Maria decided to move out on her own. The only apartment she could afford was in a substandard building. "My father forbade me to live there, and my mother threatened to have a heart attack. The only other option was moving in with Jim, which really would have killed her. So I stayed."

Despite her family's opposition, Maria kept writing. "The more they disapproved of me, the more I needed to write to remind myself of who I am. It's the only thing I do well, and if I had stopped I would have disappeared completely. Fortunately, nobody in the family takes me very seriously, so they weren't as angry as they might have been. It was depressing, though. My father started referring to me as his 'hopeless daughter.'"

When Maria first brought Jim home, her parents distrusted him. "He was Anglo, and I'd met him in that crazy program, and that was all they needed to know," she said. But once he started law school, their attitudes changed. They began to hope he would be a stabilizing influence on a daughter they saw as flighty and backward.

Maria and Jim were married soon after Jim finished law school and got his first job, in a midsize Manhattan firm. They live in another, more upwardly mobile section of the Bronx, so Maria visits her family and old neighborhood often. Last year, Maria gave birth to a baby girl, Melissa.

Maria stays home and looks after Melissa, and she tries to write while the baby naps. "She is a source of deep inspiration to me," Maria said. "Every day she teaches me about love, patience, fear, and joy, and all of this deepens my writing and makes it richer. But I'm always tired. She's not a good sleeper, and it seems as if every time I get involved in a piece, she wakes up and starts crying. Since Jim has a 'real' job and I don't, he thinks he shouldn't have to help around the house. My mother takes care of Cecilia's children, but that's because Cecilia 'works.' She's not about to take on another child so I can waste my time on what she calls 'that nonsense.'"

Maria faces a quandary that is common among mothers who are artists. Making art is often considered a luxury, something we should happily shelve to care for our families. This is especially true if, as in Maria's case, our work is not likely to bring in money. For many of us, though, art is the medium through which we stay in touch with our deepest, most authentic selves.

As much as we love our children, meeting a small child's

needs can be draining and demoralizing, especially if nobody is helping us. This is when we most need our art to sustain us, and it's when we're least likely to find the time or energy to pursue it.

"I sometimes feel as if I'm disappearing," Maria said. "Like there's no 'me' left, only Melissa's mommy, who exists to feed her and change her diapers. I don't even look like myself—I've never lost my pregnancy weight, and I have bags under my eyes. I fight that feeling of disappearing the only way I know how—by writing. The upshot is that I find myself sitting at the computer at 3 AM, swilling coffee to stay alert enough to concentrate. Sometimes I'm so exhausted I just stare at the screen, then get up and raid the refrigerator, then the baby cries and my writing time is over, and I'm a dishrag the rest of the day.

"In the meantime, one of my friends from the creative writing program has made it big. Her novel is on all the best-seller lists, and every time I open a magazine or turn on the TV, there she is. There's going to be a movie deal, too."

Maria said she wished her friend well, but that she felt like a "loser" in comparison. Her friend is unattached and devotes all of her time to writing and promoting her book. "Plus, she's gorgeous and charming. She's a good writer, but I know one reason she's getting all this attention is that she's hot. That's not jealousy; that's just the way it is for women. And here I am, fat and shy and too tired to string two words together."

Maria cried all the way through our first interview. The derogatory terms she used to describe herself—"fat" (she was overweight, but hardly obese), "loser," "stupid," and so on—were also red flags for serious depression. I questioned her carefully about possible impulses to hurt herself or her baby, prepared to send her for an immediate psychiatric evaluation, but she didn't show any signs of suicidal or violent thoughts.

Despite her depression, there were very hopeful signs. Maria had the strength and courage to persevere with her work in the face of her parents' opposition, her own self-doubts, and the lack of time, energy, and support that she faced, and she described her situation and feelings with honesty and insight. Our task was to bring to the surface and integrate what she knew, deep inside— that she was an intelligent, insightful adult capable of producing important art. Then she would be able to use her strength and creativity to regain control of her life and work.

□ □ □

Elizabeth, Lisette, Janna, Bonnie, and Maria were born in different periods and geographical areas, to families of different economic and social classes, backgrounds, and ethnicities. As women artists, though, they have much in common. The rigid preconceptions about women's literature that convinced Elizabeth that she was not a serious artist in 1941 were still at play when Janna submitted an angry poem to her high school literary magazine in 1996. Lisette, growing up in an affluent Atlanta suburb, felt the same desperation to be allowed to practice her art as Bonnie, in poverty-stricken Appalachia, and Maria, in a drug- and crime-ridden section of the Bronx. These women also share a strong commitment to overcoming their pasts and growing as artists and as human beings. I hope that by reading their stories—both their setbacks and their triumphs—you will be inspired to explore and gain insight into your own creative process.

None of us can escape or forget our negative experiences, but as we become aware of the destructive messages that continue to influence us, the messages lose their power to sap our self-esteem and creativity. In the following exercise, you can start identifying the messages of your own childhood.

There is no right or wrong way to do this exercise or any of the exercises in this book. I've included Janna's and Maria's accounts of how the exercise worked for them to give you an idea of how each person responds differently and finds something unique in the experience. As you'll see, Bonnie declined to do the exercise because she felt it didn't apply to her. I believe everyone can benefit from examining her early experiences, but if you feel strongly that you don't want to do it, just skip the exercise and go on to the next chapter. The point isn't to make you conform to my idea of artistic health but to help spark your own creative approach to the issues that may be holding you back.

Exercise:

"girls should"

Sit in your quiet place at a time when you're not likely to be interrupted. Think about the person you consider your primary caregiver. Get a mental picture of your earliest memory of that person's face and then draw it. (Don't worry about artistic ability. The point is to connect with your memories and feelings in as many ways as possible.) Draw a large balloon coming out of the mouth. Inside the balloon, write the words GIRLS SHOULD—and then write down everything that comes to mind. Don't judge what you are writing or even think about whether it's accurate or fair. Just keep writing until you're sure there is nothing left to say. Continue the balloon on another piece of paper, if necessary.

Pay attention to any feelings that come up, as always, and note these on the page. Even more important, think about your caregiver's background, what his or her experiences may have been, how these attitudes may have been formed. You can even take it back a few generations if you have enough information.

When you're done, put the pages away for a few days. Then take them out and consider them again. Do any connections jump out between your caregiver's attitudes and your artistic blocks or inhibitions? Between these attitudes and his or her own background? Write these down, too. Don't try to use them to reason your way out of your blocks or into a premature "forgiveness" of your caregiver's failings. Don't try to argue with the caregiver's beliefs—just be aware of them.

When Maria, who felt "stupid" because her interests and abilities were more artistic than practical, did this exercise, she focused on her grandmother. "At first I wrote a lot of stuff that didn't surprise me," she said. "I wrote, 'Girls should be smart, clean their rooms, do their homework, help with the cooking,' and so on. Then I found that I'd written, '. . . color inside the lines,' and I was suddenly four years old, lying prone on the roof of our building on a sunny day, happily occupied with my coloring book while my grandmother hung the wash. I was proud of the landscape I had colored: blue cows munching orange grass against a fiery red sky.

"My grandmother walked by and reprimanded me for using the 'wrong' colors. I was crushed. I realized that a lot of my feelings of 'wrongness' come from that—not from that specific incident, but from that attitude, that there is a right and wrong way to do *everything,* even something as individual and joyous as coloring, and that if I rely on my own intuition, my choices will be wrong and embarrassing. And yet, I had done a beautiful, original thing, one that I would praise my own daughter for.

"When I did the second part of the exercise, about focusing on the caregiver, I started thinking about what it must have been like for my grandmother to come to New York for the first time as a grown woman. My father and his brother came here first, got jobs and saved money, and then sent for her. She didn't speak any English when she arrived. It was hard for everyone in my family, but especially for her, I think—she could never quite get the hang of how 'Americans' did things, and she wanted us to succeed—so of course she was preoccupied with the rules.

"Now when I get down on myself, or my work, for being wrong and weird, I think about my *abuelita.* I explain to her, in my mind, that in America it's okay to color a cow blue. That makes me laugh."

Bonnie, the photographer, didn't think there was a point to doing the exercise. She said, "What I got was indifference and neglect, and I've learned that that was better than what a lot of other girls got. At least nobody was trying to steer me in a direction I didn't want to go in. Since no one in my family cared much what I did, I didn't realize that I might have any limitations other than the ones other people put on me. I was able to take advantage of every opportunity that came my way."

If nothing comes up for you, don't push yourself. On the other hand, don't give up just because the results aren't immediate. Sometimes you need to repeat this exercise more than once to unearth memories or feelings that continue to affect you.

The first time Janna did this exercise, she drew her mother's face. "Nothing much happened," she said. "I guess we'd worked through all that. I tried my father, too, and I was able to come up with a few things he said that made me angry, but really, it felt fake, as if I were dredging for problems that didn't exist.

"Then, one day, I was working on a painting that was just wrong. The colors were wrong, the distance between the two figures, the whole feeling of the painting was off. I was angry with myself; I kept thinking, *Can't you do anything right?* I suddenly thought, *I need to do the exercise using Louis.*

"Pay dirt. I wrote, 'Girls should do what I tell them to do.'

"At first I was just in a rage at him. All I could think of was that he had ruined our lives, stolen our childhood. I had fantasies of 'visiting' him in prison and shooting him there. Crazy stuff. I couldn't work."

When Janna told me this, I suggested that she write Louis a letter describing her feelings in detail, and then put the letter away.

"I wrote him a twenty-page letter. Everything came out—even how much I hated the dirt under his fingernails, and now when I see a man with dirty nails I want to throw up. I told him I wanted to see him die. It was hard to put it in a drawer and not mail it.

"When we talked about it, though, I realized I didn't want to have any contact with him at all, not even to hurt him. I just wanted him out of my head. So one afternoon when my sister, Elaine, was visiting, we burned the letter, and my drawing of him, in the bathroom sink. Then we walked to a neighborhood park, buried the ashes, and spat on the grave.

"Afterward, I was able to get back to that painting. I realized I'd been treating it the way Louis treated me—contemptuously, as I sometimes do with my work, trying to force it to do what I wanted instead of having patience with the process, with what was bubbling up."

Like Janna, you may need to make a few "false starts" before the origin of a block becomes apparent, or you may wish to explore the messages of several important adults in your early life. In the weeks and months ahead, take your drawing and notes out and look at them every week or so. When you find yourself feeling blocked, consider whether you are "listening" to the caregiver in your drawing, or perhaps to a different one. If a different one, repeat the exercise using that caregiver. Get used to connecting self-doubt and creative inhibitions with specific messages from your childhood, and get used to detoxifying these messages by considering the source.

Young children nearly always believe what their parents, teachers, and other caregivers say. It's part of survival—if we distrusted our elders and doubted their wisdom and judgment, we wouldn't learn the basics of self-care that later allow us to live independent lives. For the world to feel safe and make sense to us, we need to believe that these adults are strong, intelligent people, capable of guiding us through the complications and dangers of life. That trust makes us vulnerable, though. When what they communicate to us is that we're wrong, frivolous, stupid, or bad, either we swallow the message whole, or we develop deep conflicts about our self-worth and whether others can be trusted.

Our siblings' and peers' approval is important to us, too, and helps us define our place in the world. When they shun, belittle, or bully us, we often feel unlikable or deficient. And all of this has a negative impact on our ability to create with confidence and spontaneity.

These conflicts and distorted beliefs often last long after we've forgotten how they began. Identifying their source is one important step in ridding ourselves of their power. Another is to recognize and align ourselves with the people who have nourished and supported our art, our ambitions, and our most authentic selves. That's what the next chapter is about.

i want
to be
you

the importance of role

models to our

creative lives

Chapter Two

Often, in talking about their childhoods, artistic clients reveal deep sources of pain and discouragement—Janna's experience of abuse; Bonnie's extreme poverty; the racism that formed the background of Lisette's youth; or parents who were unable to care for them because of alcoholism, depression, or other forms of mental illness, to name just a few problems. To get a sense of these women's strengths, I ask, "What was it that enabled you to survive your childhood and to achieve as much as you have?" Almost invariably, the answer includes a role model—an individual who figured heavily in the client's life, and whose own life served as a beacon. It may have been an adventurous aunt whose independence gave the client a taste of a life rich in choices, or a schoolteacher who took an interest in a gifted, needy child. Whoever the role model is, it seems evident that for many creative women the presence of a strong, successful woman in their lives has been critical in empowering them to pursue their own paths.

For years, though, I was at a loss to describe any role models of my own. Nearly all of the women in my family of origin were homemakers who were opposed to the idea of careers for women, and who subscribed to very conventional beliefs about gender roles, including the propriety of the wife's subservience to her husband. One of my aunts was a buyer for a department store, but this was by default—she was a widow with two young children and the object of much pity (and not a lot of help) from the rest of the family.

I did have some excellent teachers who liked and praised me—I was smart and generally well behaved—but none who particularly took me under her wing. And I knew no artists of any sort when I was growing up. No one encouraged me to blaze my own trail; no one, in Maria's words, ever gave me permission to color outside the lines or even showed me that this was possible.

I believe this absence of role models was one factor in the delayed onset of my writing career. I wasn't encouraged to think of my life as something I could shape myself or to see my writing ability as anything but a skill that could be useful in conveying others' ideas.

And yet, during all the years when I was editing, speechwriting, and studying, a part of me felt false—felt I was living someone else's life. That deep, wise part of me knew *exactly* how I wanted to live and what I wanted to accomplish. I didn't think about this often—I kept myself very busy and tended to push what I considered idle fantasy to the back of my mind—but when I was doing research in the library, I would find my mind wandering from the psychology stacks over to the fiction section, imagining that I could spend all day reading novels and writing stories of my own. I would read the **New York Times Book Review** with a combination of eagerness and despair, hoping to find interesting books to read and, at the same time, feeling disconsolate in the knowledge that mine would never be among them, that I was permanently (so I thought) sidelined.

Where did this come from, this sense of another, more authentic life? When I did the exercise at the end of this chapter, a figure popped into my consciousness—one I hadn't thought about in years. **Betsy Ray.**

Betsy was the creation of Maud Hart Lovelace. In a series of autobiographical novels for children and young adults, Lovelace traced Betsy's life and career from the age of four through marriage and motherhood. The earlier books are storybooks for young readers, and the later ones are high-quality teen romances, enabling the dedicated reader (as I was) to "grow up" along with Betsy.

What sets Betsy apart from other fictional heroines whose stories I loved is that she plans, from a very early age, to be a writer. Her family and friends support this ambition, and as the stories continue, Betsy goes on to win writing competitions in high school and then to become a published author. Her high school boyfriend, Joe, whom she later marries, is also a budding writer, and the two help one another to realize their dreams.

As a child, I read biographies of women writers when I could find them, because even then I was interested in the "story behind the story"—who was the person behind the curtain, pulling the strings? I didn't find them inspiring, though—rather, they intimidated me. Many books for young readers at that time incorporated moral lessons about kindness, honesty, and strength in adversity that were meant to inspire but that instead made their heroines seem saintly or unusually strong and able. I admired them but didn't dare to think I could emulate them. I didn't believe I could ever "write my way out of poverty" by sheer strength of will, as Louisa May Alcott had done; I was sure I didn't have Nellie Bly's physical courage or the unswerving moral compass of Harriet Beecher Stowe. The actual conflicts and complications of these women's lives, their failures of nerve and imagination, and their ambivalence and frustrations—all of which could have been instructive to an aspiring writer in search of role models—were smoothed over, removing their achievements from the possibility of attainment by a mere mortal.

Betsy, on the other hand, was a real little girl. She was embarrassed about the gap between her front teeth. She fought with her sister, she despaired of ever mastering algebra, and she almost failed high school science after procrastinating for too long on a final project. She weathered misunderstandings with friends and a crush on a "bad boy" who focused his charm and affections on her friend. She was an indifferent athlete and a hopelessly clumsy ice skater. She felt bored and lost in college and ended up dropping out. Except that she was growing up in turn-of-the-twentieth-century "Deep Valley" (Mankato), Minnesota, she could have been my friend. Her example seemed to suggest that a regular, fallible girl, who wasn't necessarily a genius, a saint, or a superhero, could grow up to be a writer—and the fact that Lovelace had based Betsy's life on her own made the stories doubly encouraging.

It was as though I had carried Betsy's example around with

me for years, just waiting for someone—Betsy's parents?—to give me permission to apply it to my own life. And, in an odd way, Betsy did introduce me to my first flesh-and-blood writing mentor.

Four weeks after completing my psychology PhD. program, in the summer of 1994, I gave birth to my son, Ben. By this time, I had acknowledged to myself that I did, indeed, want to write. I started reading systematically—books by women, books about women writers, books about the psychology of writing—with the intention of overcoming my inhibitions and learning to write from my deepest self. I was haunted by one story idea in particular—I wrote and rewrote the opening pages but never progressed further than that. The need to juggle my new career and the demands of an energetic child pushed my ambition to the back burner—or at least, that's what I told myself.

Then, in October of 1997, Lovelace's daughter, Merian Kirchner, died. Her obituary in the **New York Times** mentioned that Merian had been active on an Internet chat room for fans of her mother's writing. Intrigued, I logged on to the site and discovered a community of interesting, literate women, all of whom had been inspired, as writers or readers, by the stories about Betsy Ray.

I found myself drawn into conversation repeatedly with one particular group member. We discovered common tastes in literature for both adults and children. We were both first-time parents of young children, and we compared stories, tips, and reading material. We took our friendship offline, first exchanging emails and then arranging to meet.

Her name was Michelle Herman. She was, and is, a wonderful novelist, essayist, and short story writer. She teaches in the MFA program in creative writing at the Ohio State University.

At first, I was thrilled just to meet a real writer. Michelle was my first. After several months of rereading and discussing Lovelace's stories, though, Betsy's spirit of adventure infected me once again. I screwed up my courage and asked Michelle: If I could manage to finish the story I had been working on for three years, would she be willing to read it and tell me what she thought? She responded, "Of course!"

I panicked. I felt as though judgment day had arrived. I was tempted to find new excuses to put off finishing the story, possibly forever. But another part of me realized that this was the opportunity I had been waiting for, possibly all my life. For weeks, I forced myself to sit at my desk after work, writing a page a night before going home. I wrote on the bus, and sometimes in the bathroom. I awoke early, before Ben, and typed into the computer the copy I'd scrawled the previous day.

When I realized I was rewriting for the sake of not finishing—that I was not improving the manuscript and was, in some cases, making it worse—I had to admit that I was done. I emailed it to Michelle and prayed that if she hated it she would still want to be friends with me.

A week later, I received a marked-up copy of my story in the mail. She had made comments on every paragraph, on nearly every sentence, about awkward word choices, choppy transitions, and unnecessary information. I was thrilled: She had treated my work as a piece of copy that was worth her professional attention. I still have the marked-up manuscript. I treasure it as the manifestation of the day I felt I was initiated into the guild. And, even more, I treasure her closing comment: "You have what it takes." I still tear up now, writing that. I was forty-five years old, and no one had ever said that to me before. I had never given anyone the chance.

Of course, it wasn't Michelle who gave me permission to be a writer, or Betsy's parents, or Maud Hart Lovelace. I had to give myself that permission, to decide that I wanted this badly enough to risk being judged by someone whose opinion mattered to me, and to decide that my work was worth her time. And I hope that if Michelle had hated my story and advised me to stick to writing case notes, I would have persisted anyway. But the Betsy stories had set the stage for this great leap of mine—just knowing that a little girl who was no smarter or better than I was had sat dreaming in a library a century before, and had been able to realize those dreams through trial and error, helped me to imagine that I, too, had the right to these dreams; and Michelle showed me the next step on my path. That is what role models do for us.

A positive role model, whether we encounter her in real life or in the pages of a book, can serve as a counterweight to the messages that bog us down. Some role models give us material assistance, as Bonnie's photography teacher, Frank, did. Others help us just by existing and doing the things our family or community tells us are wrong or impossible for us. They help us see that there is another way to live our lives and inspire us to pursue our own paths.

Lisette, whom we met in the previous chapter, grew up unaware of role models in her field. "It wasn't that women composers led lives I couldn't emulate—I didn't even know they existed," she said. "I admired my mother, and several other strong women of color, a great deal, but their lives always seemed so indirect to me—they used their prodigious strength and competence to further the aims of their men or to better their children's lives. These are admirable goals, don't get me wrong, but they weren't what I wanted for myself. My heart was in music, not in domestic life.

"Our family worshipped Dr. Martin Luther King. Coretta Scott King was often held up to me as a role model worth emulating—a brilliant thinker, and a real lady, who devoted her life to peace and social justice.

"Now that I'm safely ensconced in my own profession, I can better appreciate what a remarkable woman King was. But back then, I hated and resented her. I saw her as a gifted musician who had abandoned a promising career to serve her husband and children, and whose goodness was always being shoved down my throat as a rebuke to my selfishness and my unwomanly aspirations."

Coretta Scott King served as a negative role model for Lisette, not because King herself was deficient in some way, but because her example, held up for Lisette to emulate, instead made her feel her own ambitions were inappropriate and selfish.

Janna, the painter, was also exposed to a negative role model: "Lisa Kirkland, the school's 'real' artist. She was a gentle, ethereal girl who painted sensitive still lifes, often in watercolor. Goldfish in a bowl, a glass of wine, a vase of flowers, that sort of thing. She had long golden hair and wore these flowing, artsy dresses, fringed shawls, and dangling, beaded earrings. Everyone loved her and her work. She won all the prizes, and the teachers made a big fuss over her, wrote glowing recommendations to the major art schools. She made me want to puke. There was nothing real about her, or her work, at all. Nothing challenging or dangerous. Her paintings belonged on greeting cards, and she was like some TV actress playing an Artist. Everyone thought she was hot stuff, and that I should try to be more like her."

Fortunately, Janna had a powerful positive role model at home: "My mom. She always gave both my sister and me the idea that we could do anything we wanted. Not only didn't she force us to conform to some stereotypical 'feminine' image, but—and I think this is rarer—she encouraged us to make our own choices, no matter how far they diverged from her own. Maybe she wanted us to be doctors, but she never showed it. So I became a radical lesbian painter, and my sister is a housewife who homeschools her kids—and our mother totally supports both of us.

"I didn't know about other women artists when I was a child, because I was a generally ignorant and self-absorbed kid and I had no idea that I wanted to be an artist myself. But my mom encouraged our creativity, and thinking for ourselves, and she lived out these qualities in her own professional life."

Like Janna, stand-up comedian Christina Martin found a role model within her own family: "My grandmother left home at sixteen and married a jazz pianist. She then accompanied him as a jazz singer in the clubs around London. I always admired her. She just saw a life for herself outside of the usual. That's what I want, too."

In thinking about role models in her own field, Martin says: "There are so few female comics to aspire to that my role models have been male by default, my main inspirations being Bill Hicks, Lenny Bruce, Eddie Izzard, and Stewart Lee. One thing I noticed as I compiled this list was the fact that all of these men are outsiders.

"I may have gravitated toward them not only because they are/were great comics but also because they embody an experience common to female comics—that of having to work hard to be accepted or effect a change.

"Lenny Bruce struggled against obscenity laws and ultimately lost his life in the struggle to express himself. Bill Hicks dedicated his short life to changing people's attitudes with his challenging and thought-provoking stand-up. Stewart Lee has continued this struggle with his uncompromising form of comedy and nightly runs the risk of playing to the confused silence of a crowd expecting a 'joke blower' and not understanding what he is doing. Eddie Izzard very bravely goes onstage in drag and uses comedy to tackle ignorance.

"When I go onstage I face the struggle of overcoming a female stereotype and the resistance the crowd will sometimes put up because of this. I was inspired by these comics to take on this challenge and to continue with the struggle even when it seems too hard to face."

Martin and Janna looked to the women in their families for examples of strength and courage. Like me, Elizabeth had to find hers in fiction. "Jo March inspired me," Elizabeth told me. "I didn't want to be her—I wanted her sister Amy's nice house, handsome husband, and life of luxury—but I loved it that she 'scribbled.' I wanted her to be my sister, too. And I didn't give two hoots about Louisa May Alcott and her noble, self-abnegating life. I tried not to think about her except to look for her name on the spines of books. I didn't want to know that there were people making these stories up, people I may not have liked. There were enough people I didn't want to deal with in my everyday life—I didn't want them invading my fantasy life, too!"

It's wonderful when a positive role model is a constant presence in our day-to-day lives, guiding and inspiring us. Janna confides in her mother and consults her about many important aspects of her art and life. Those of us who, like Elizabeth and Lisette, aren't lucky enough to find these exemplars at home or in our communities have to use our creativity to discover them. That's what the following exercise is designed to help you do.

When Hillary Clinton was first lady, she was widely ridiculed after Bob Woodward reported in his book, *The Choice*, that she "channeled" her role model, Eleanor Roosevelt, to help her make decisions. The implication was that Clinton was basing important life choices on imagined communications with Roosevelt that she received through séances and incantations.

What she was actually doing was a common exercise for unleashing inner wisdom through contacting the parts of her personality that identified with her role model. Nothing is spooky or supernatural about this, and it doesn't entail rapping on tables or communicating with the dead.

Exercise:

unleashing your inner wisdom

Sit in a comfortable position at a time when you are not likely to be interrupted. Check your breath to be sure you are breathing deeply from your diaphragm. Do a mental scan of your body to identify any areas of tightness, and direct these areas to relax.

Shut your eyes, if you feel comfortable doing so. If not, stare at an unadorned space—perhaps the ceiling or floor. Try to visualize a beautiful, comfortable setting—someplace you have been before, where you felt safe and connected, or perhaps a place of your imagination. Experience it as specifically as you can, through as many senses as possible: Notice what is under your feet—grass? Sand? A thick rug? What time of year is it, and what time of day? What are the colors and smells? Is there a breeze? Some people find that drawing the scene makes it easier to pin down.

As you become accustomed to this place, notice that you're not alone. Walking toward you is an intelligent, benevolent presence, whose form becomes clearer with every step.

When you recognize this person, just take a few minutes to absorb her or his identity and presence. Take in as many details as possible—clothing, facial expressions and body language, particular scents or sounds.

Imagine that this person has something of enormous importance to tell you and that the two of you can communicate telepathically. Write down whatever words spring into your mind, whether they make sense or not.

Ask your role model questions. Write down the "answers"—again, even if they seem nonsensical. Later, when you look them over, you may find that they relate to your life and work in unexpected and important ways.

Before ending this exercise, you may wish to thank your role model. Then, very slowly, return your attention to present reality, noticing the details of the room and considering your agenda for the coming day. Put the written answers away for a day or two. Then, again at a quiet time, take them out and see whether they resonate for you in your current situation. If not, try again in a week or two.

Some women tell me about specific information or guidance they receive from their inner role models. Many report an even more helpful aspect of the exercise: the feeling that they have found or rediscovered a friend. When we feel unsupported by our family or community, it can help to identify or recall strong, wise women who can accompany us on our journey into deeper self-knowledge and artistic growth.

For example, Maria reported, "I started to draw a pretty, cozy living room, but it turned into my elementary school art room, and then I was 'visited' by Mrs. Núñez, my art teacher from first through third grades. I hadn't thought about her in years, and I never considered her that way before, but suddenly it all came back—she would wear open-toed sandals with pantyhose, and a cotton smock like a nurse. She, and the room, always smelled like tempera paint and clay. She would have us paint pictures from our imaginations, getting as sloppy and enthusiastic as we liked, and then if we wanted to, we could tell her what they were about. I would make up stories to go along with my crazy pictures, and she loved them. She would always ask, 'And what happened after that? And then?' I got the idea that what was in my head was important and worth putting out in the world.

"After I did the exercise, I looked her up in real life. She's still teaching at my old school, and I visited her there. She was amazed that I remembered her, and she was happy to hear how I've made use of what she taught me.

"In the exercise, I asked her how to get past this feeling of being wrong and stupid because I don't always think in a linear way. She said, 'You are Einstein.' I had no idea what that meant.

"But later I remembered reading that Einstein was thought to be mentally retarded when he was young because he didn't do things the same way other children did—and that even as an adult, he was always odd and unconventional. I don't think I'm Einstein, but it's good to keep in mind that 'normal' doesn't always mean 'better.'

"I don't think the real Mrs. Núñez would have answered my question that way—in fact, I don't think she would know what to do with such a question. It doesn't matter. There was a Mrs. Núñez inside me all this time, just waiting to be contacted. Now I go back to that art room in my head and talk to her sometimes.

Jim and my family would think I was nuts if I told them what I was doing, but it really helps me to sort out my thoughts this way, with a safe, encouraging friend, who is, of course, me."

Lisette visualized her summer camp. "It was a beautiful, woodsy place, with primitive cabins, a lake, singing around the campfire. I loved it there, and I loved the friends I made there. So I wasn't surprised that that was the place that came to mind right away.

"I imagined sitting outside by the lake, as I often did when I was there, just staring into the water and dreaming my dreams.

"When the figure appeared, it was tall and thin, and I thought at first it must be a counselor who had been especially kind to me. But then, as she got closer, I realized it was Harriet Tubman!

"Harriet Tubman defied not just white slave owners and lawmakers, but her own husband, to seek her freedom and help others to freedom and safety. She sang her own song, always.

"I asked her where to go from here, and she said, 'Listen to the music.'

"I'm still figuring out what that means. At first, I took it literally to mean that my future lies in more of the same, listening to music, making music. And I do believe that.

"But lately, I've found myself humming that old song, 'Follow the Drinking Gourd,' about the slaves' passage to freedom, and the old man waiting by the river's edge to carry them to safety. And I've been thinking about how Harriet lived, not only for herself, but for others as well—about how many people she helped—saved, really—through her Underground Railroad work, and then, later, as a nurse. She could serve others without compromising herself, because she knew who she was, and she had confidence in her strength.

"I've always tried to be a good teacher, but lately I've been concentrating more on identifying promising students, especially women and minorities, and giving them the same leg up my college mentor gave me. It's important to give back, just not at the cost of sacrificing my deepest self.

"And, of course, the Underground Railroad didn't run just on Harriet Tubman's steam. Every person in that network trusted and depended on every other person. One weak link and the chain would have broken.

"So I think the other meaning of the message is that I need to experience myself as part of a network of musicians, and women, and people of color, living and dead—that I need to develop myself as an individual, but I also need to learn to take wisdom from my elders and pass it on to my students and to others. That we're not alone, that we don't have to do this alone."

□ □ □

Creating art tends to be a solitary pursuit. Even when we're productive and successful, we often feel isolated. When we're stuck, we can feel as though we've been dumped in a strange and hostile country without a map. A role model can help us understand how we got here, guide us through this new territory, and keep us company along the way.

As you revisit your early successes and, especially, failures while reading the next chapter, keep your inner role model in mind. If you find yourself becoming angry or upset while reliving a painful episode, talk to her about it. Ask her for insight, advice, or just a hand on your shoulder. Be open to her presence and guidance. This wisdom and support is always there, inside you, waiting for you. As Lisette said, you're not alone.

getting
our toes
wet

early artistic

successes

and failures

Chapter Three

i have a horrible confession to make: I am a plagiarist. Shocking, but true. I plagiarized my first short story. I would like to say that I wasn't aware of what I was doing—that I had read the story and forgotten about it, that it lodged somewhere in my unconscious and poured out of me as though it were my own, that the realization of my accidental theft shocked and surprised me. That wasn't the case, though. I knew perfectly well that I was lifting another writer's work and that this was wrong. I knew because my first-grade teacher had explained this to me the week before, when I had turned in "Humpty Dumpty" as an original poem.

Before that, it hadn't occurred to me that stories and poems were the property of anyone in particular. Mrs. Latouchie, my teacher, straightened me out about that. She had instructed my reading group—the Robins, which everyone knew was the smartest group—to write a poem about an object we would find in our homes. I thought the assignment was laughably easy. There were always eggs in our refrigerator. I dashed off "Humpty Dumpty" and ostentatiously flipped through my workbook as Marion and Jimmy, my fellow group members, sweated it out.

Later that day, Mrs. Latouchie called me up to her desk. "I am deeply disappointed in you, Susan," she said sadly.

I was a model student—a strong, early reader and an adult

pleaser. I didn't know what I'd done wrong, but the thought of disappointing Mrs. Latouchie, whom I adored, was devastating. I burst into tears.

Taking my tears as an admission of guilt, Mrs. Latouchie explained, gently but firmly, that signing one's own name to another's work was called plagiarism, and that it was a crime.

Mrs. Latouchie was a kind, motherly person, and I know she meant only to guide me back onto what she saw as the path of honesty. She certainly didn't intend to spark a vision of all the king's horses and all the king's men parading into the classroom to nab my seven-year-old criminal self and throw her in prison. But, like most children my age, I had no sense of proportion.

A child's capacity for abstract thinking doesn't develop fully until adolescence (if then). Before that, kids are liable to interpret exaggerations, figures of speech, and throwaway comments in a literal, serious way, especially when they come from a trusted adult. For example, several of my clients can recall being called "idiot" or "liar" by a parent. As adults, these women understand that their parents were just expressing frustration about a broken figurine or a fib told to avoid punishment. At the time, though, they swallowed these comments whole and started to think of themselves as stupid or dishonest.

In my experience, highly imaginative children—those who will later be drawn to creative work—are even more vulnerable to being affected in a lasting way by a chance remark. Many creative people are imagistic thinkers—our minds attach vivid pictures and sensations to ordinary figures of speech. Maria, the poet and short story writer, remembers hearing her mother mention that an uncle had been fired from his job. Five-year-old Maria, who hadn't heard the term "fired" before, began crying uncontrollably at the mental picture of her beloved Uncle Carlos in flames. Even after her parents reassured her that Carlos had merely lost his job, she was haunted by this image. More than twenty years later, there is still a slight shudder along with her laugh as she tells the story.

So, as silly as it sounds now, my first-grade self really believed I had accidentally committed a criminal act.

Mrs. Latouchie took pity on me. She took "my" poem and, winking at me, ripped it up and dropped it into the metal wastebasket next to her desk. "We'll just pretend this never happened," she said. "A smart girl like you can certainly write her own poem. You don't need to copy from anybody! In fact, I expect wonderful things from you! Don't let me down, now."

Her words, intended to reassure me, made the situation even worse. I felt paralyzed—my first experience of writer's block.

Up to that moment, I had never imagined that writing could be dangerous. I made up songs all the time, about everything— my dachshund's wiggly torso, the color of mashed potatoes with peas smushed into them, Snow White. My father and I had even made one up about Mrs. Latouchie (in which she danced the hootchie-kootchie and walked her little poochie). But I knew, in that instant, that if she ordered me to go back to my desk and write an original poem, I would not be able to do it. Every word now felt fraught with the possibility of doing something dreadfully wrong or deeply disappointing.

So the following week, when she told the Robins to write a one-page story, I froze. Mrs. Latouchie was expecting me to come up with something wonderful, and I knew I had nothing wonderful in me. I stared at the blank page. It was a minefield. Any word I wrote could explode.

This time, Jimmy and Marion scribbled away happily while I gripped my pencil so tightly it broke. I could not think of anything to write about that would be "wonderful." Everything about my home life seemed boring and stupid. Mrs. Latouchie knew all about school. I couldn't write a fairy tale, because that would be a crime. I was one panicky little girl.

Finally, as she was about to collect the papers, I remembered a story I had read in a comic book.

In the 1950s, many comic books included one or two very short and simple pure-text stories, usually with morally uplifting themes, I assume as a sop to parents and teachers who tended to condemn the books as "junk." I may have been the only child in America who actually read these stories.

The story that popped into my head was about a little rose who believes she is ugly and stinky because she is planted in a vegetable garden and the vegetables make fun of her. Finally she meets another flower, and they become friends.

I made a quick and desperate calculation that Mrs. Latouchie was unlikely to read *Wendy the Good Little Witch* comics, and I wrote down what I remembered of the story.

Mrs. Latouchie loved it. She told me how proud she was of my originality. "See?" she said. "I told you you could do it!" But I knew I could never have thought up such a good story.

Mrs. Latouchie was so happy with my work that she posted the story in the hallway outside our classroom for everyone to read.

I spent the week or so before the story was taken down in a state of breathless agitation. I jumped whenever I was spoken to. I had my first experience of insomnia—I lay awake imagining that one of the older kids would recognize the story and turn me in. Since this was my second offense, I assumed I would go to jail for a long time. At the very least, I would be kicked out of school.

As frightening as those prospects were, they paled beside my primary fear: letting everyone down. I imagined my parents and Mrs. Latouchie all regarding me with deep disappointment and the sad realization that their trust in me, to come up with something wonderful all by myself, had been misplaced. I would rather be thrown in jail, I felt, than endure that.

In the end, there were no external consequences. Someone added a missing "the" to the story, but otherwise it went uncommented on, and after a few weeks it was taken down and returned to me for safekeeping. At home, I followed Mrs. Latouchie's example and ripped the page to pieces. I slept through the night for the first time since writing it.

This may seem overwrought to you, certainly an exaggeration of a long-ago childhood event, right? Wrong. Because, though I can see the humor in it now, that wasn't the case at the time. As many children do, I took a not-terribly-noteworthy reprimand and blew it up into World War III proportions.

Like Maria, who imagined her "fired" uncle in flames, I both laugh and cringe when I recall this episode. And for a long time, when I looked back on it, the very fact that it seemed so slight and silly, so unworthy of losing sleep over, kept me from realizing that it had affected my feelings about writing in a deep and lasting way.

I didn't understand the extent of its impact until I was designing the original version of the exercise at the end of this chapter for a client. I test-drove it, as I do with all new exercises, and suddenly it was 1959 again. It's hard to write about, even now, without reexperiencing those sweaty palms and that trapped, desperate feeling. But it was an important discovery, both for the light it shed on my own creative blocks and because it helped me to understand, in a visceral way, how seemingly innocuous incidents can have a surprisingly strong and tenacious impact on a child's self-image.

Another reason the experience stayed with me, of course, was that, even at seven, I had begun to think of myself as a writer. And this was my first negative critique, my first inkling that something I wrote could be read with anything but approval and delight.

When we first begin creating (or, in my case, copying) art, we're very sensitive to the responses we get. Ideally, of course, all art would be the pure expression of our deepest selves, regardless of anyone else's opinion. Some children are actually encouraged to obey the creative promptings of their own hearts. Janna, the painter who is an abuse survivor, feels lucky in this regard. "Fortunately, nobody ever expected me to do anything creative until I landed in therapy," she told me. "Our school system was very conservative, very 3-Rs and sports minded. We were rewarded for writing mindless, derivative drivel, as long as it was spelled correctly and in proper paragraph form. Art class consisted of memorizing the color wheel, or drawing a vase of daisies the teacher set out, as 'realistically' as possible.

"It sounds dreary, and it was, but it was also helpful, I think. I never took any of those assignments too seriously, so when Nina, the therapist, suggested that I express my feelings through art, there was nothing standing between me and the work. My technique was lousy to nonexistent, but I was able to capture my authentic emotions directly. That has been a huge advantage to me. I've been able to pick up some technical expertise—at least in visual art; I'm still a pretty terrible writer—by taking classes and working with other artists, but the technique has always been in the service of what I'm trying to express and never an end in itself."

Reviews of Janna's paintings—even the negative ones—often refer to their power, intensity, and authenticity. She is also one of the few women artists I've worked with who has never considered modifying her techniques or subject matter to accommodate the market, despite vociferous opposition to some of her work. Because her first meaningful experience of art was as a vehicle for self-expression—and because her therapist wisely refrained from judging Janna's painting by any other standard, even though her talent must have been obvious—Janna has never wavered in her conviction that she is entitled, even obligated, to translate her inner vision so directly onto the canvas.

Most budding artists, though, aren't encouraged to ignore external standards when they're just starting out. Instead, their teachers, family members, and other influential adults make pronouncements about their work based on their own ideas of what constitutes "good" or "appropriate" art. These early evaluations can have a lasting influence.

All children are vulnerable to the opinions of important adults, of course. But girls, especially, are set up by our culture to want to please. This was certainly true in my childhood, and my younger clients report that, in spite of all the advances we've made, it's still true. Girls are still encouraged to spend time and money on clothes, manicures, hairstyles, and makeup. Overt sexuality is emphasized now, even for very young girls, rather than the more conservative look that was the norm for my peers, but the message is the same—looks are critically important. Books and magazine articles directed at girls continue to offer tips on achieving popularity, being a good conversationalist, and decoding boys' communications. The objective, still, is to learn how to be attractive—to present an appearance and personality that are pleasing to others. So girls tend to take criticism especially hard and are more apt to judge their work by others' standards.

Up until the "plagiarism" incidents, reading and writing had been, for me, pure pleasure. Perhaps just as important, it was acceptable for a girl to be good at them. (Back then, the common wisdom was that girls excelled at language arts until high school, when boys caught up and then surpassed them. Thus, there was no conflict, at this age, between being a good reader and writer and being a good little girl. In fact, my mother and her friends had even expressed surprise that there was a boy in my reading group, and I got the impression that they didn't think much of him.) So, for the period between ages four, when I learned to read, and seven, I was an avid and ambitious reader and writer.

I don't think I was unusual in this. Maria, as we saw in a previous chapter, sailed through her elementary years, running into academic trouble only later. The early grades tend to reward people-pleasing skills—neatness, cooperation, good listening, and the desire and ability to meet external demands. As we have seen, most girls are socialized to excel in these areas.

Mrs. Latouchie's disappointment in my innocent mistake blew down my entire house of straw. Writing didn't feel natural and joyful anymore. When I tried to write a story or poem, I would agonize over each word, afraid that it wasn't sufficiently "wonderful"—that it was stupid or boring. Is it any wonder that I've dedicated a good part of my adult career to understanding and addressing creative blocks? Mine started at the tender age of seven!

erapy, she criticized herself for being "thin-skinned."
"At my age, and with a solid career, I shouldn't worry
bout what people think. And in the composing stage,
ust me and the music, I don't care. I don't even think
one else. But as soon as I decide something is ready—
, that I need to hear it performed before I can make that
—I panic."

n she first came to see me, Lisette characterized her
 as "fear of rejection," but we both soon realized that
e complicated than that. A few weeks into therapy, she
o her anxiety about an upcoming performance of one of
ositions. I asked her to revisit her experience of playing
iece for her family. As we talked, she recalled that what
 her most wasn't her parents' refusal to give her piano
ut their amused condescension.

father basically patted me on the head and laughed.
, my mother used to humiliate me by directing me to
ittle song' for company—and when I did, the adults'
as also, 'Isn't she cute?' Believe me, if my brother had
at piece, it would have been hailed as a work of genius.
ted that feeling, of putting my deepest self out there
 patronized," she said. "And, of course, as a child, you
ense of nuance, of context. I didn't know you could be
and funny and also be taken seriously—at least, I knew
 men, presidents and so on, could accomplish this, but
one like me."

Because children tend to believe that the fate of the universe hinges on their actions—and, as you can see, I was a very
intense and serious kid—this struggle felt like life and death. If I
did manage to write something that interested others, I worried
that it might not actually be my own idea—and since it's practically impossible to come up with a totally original idea, I always
felt I was about to be pulled into the vortex of a life of crime. Yet,
deep inside, I still wanted to write.

So I found a way to keep writing. Though it wasn't the health-
iest course, it did allow me to build many of the skills a writer
needs. I began paying very careful attention to what my teachers
wanted, starting with Mrs. Latouchie. She had approved of "my"
story about the rose, so I wrote more stories about flowers and
friendships. When she suggested that I expand—maybe include a
boy in a story, or set my story somewhere else—I would do that. I
became adept at reading the assignment behind the assignment,
the unarticulated expectations. That way I was sure of pleasing
my audience, and, because I was following others' leads, I didn't
worry so much about "copying." My writing was "original" in that
I came up with my own ideas, based on what I thought they
wanted—rather like a medieval artist serving a patron.

This ability to divine and meet others' needs served me
well in school, and into adulthood, when I wrote speeches and
fund-raising material for others. It has certainly helped me in my
efforts to understand the hidden desires and conflicts that underlie many of my clients' artistic blocks. But it limited my ability to

produce authentic art—work that emanated from the depths of my being. In fact, my constant focus on what other people wanted was keeping me from even recognizing my own ideas and feelings, much less expressing them in writing.

After I realized how I was cheating myself by spending all of my energy this way, I embarked on a long, often painful course of "unlearning"—one that I'm still just beginning. And to this day—including every time I begin a new chapter of this book—my first response to the idea of writing something original, without clear guidelines or models, is, "I couldn't possibly do that!"

I can, though. I write poems and stories. I write my advice column, "The Doctor Is In," every week. And now I'm writing this book. The reactions to our early efforts may affect us deeply, but they don't have to define our relationship to our work. As I continue my own process of unlearning, I help my clients to explore the ways they were influenced by the responses to their own youthful artwork.

In the previous chapter, we saw how Maria reconnected with her elementary school art teacher through the Unleashing Your Inner Wisdom exercise. When we discussed early influences on her work, this teacher was at the top of her list. "Mrs. Núñez was so encouraging about my stories," she told me. "She gave me confidence that what others saw as crazy—my weird way of looking at the world—was valuable, at least to certain, special people.

"If my family had thought creative writing was important, they would have tried to straighten me out, to make me write regular,

realistic stories. And, knowing m
them. Instead, after Mrs. Núñez,
until I was in college, and then I
program with supportive teachers
with my feeling that everything I w
that's who I am—because that's v

Maria is learning, as I had to
work as just that—opinions. So
tant things to teach us—they m
we are blind to because we're too
don't have enough training or e
good ideas about new directions
to evaluate their suggestions an
us achieve our own goals.

Lisette, the composer you
tect herself and her work from c
though, not by developing conf
strenuously keeping her work to
composition before it was abso
ticipated in the working groups tl
the idea of collaboration was ar
hated being in the room when
heard her work for the first time
myself with alcohol and asked m
my compositions," she said, "I do
play my work for a living soul—n

In th
She said,
so much
when it's
about any
or, at leas
decision—

Whe
sensitivity
it was mo
brought u
her comp
her first p
had upset
lessons b

"My
Afterward
play my "
reaction
written th

"I ha
and being
have no s
charming
that white
not some

Lisette wasn't suffering from fear of rejection—she was afraid of being diminished as a person, and as a serious artist, if she made herself vulnerable to others' reactions. Like me, she had found a way of pursuing her art that allowed her to sidestep her fears—but now she was discovering, as I had, that working around her issues, rather than addressing them, was limiting.

"I think I come off as kind of spiky," she said. "My colleagues and students respect me, but I'm not one of the people who gets invited when a group goes out for a beer or to a ball game. I'm a loyal friend but not an easy one—I'm sensitive to slights, real and imagined. I think men are intimidated by me. I've never dated much, and the men I've been involved with have had intimacy issues of their own. I'm doing the work I want to do; my career is flourishing—but I'm starting to realize I've paid a very heavy price."

Fortunately, our attitudes and behavior are not set in stone. Our artists' imaginations may have made us more vulnerable to discouraging messages, but we can use the same imaginative ability to help undo the damage. Revisiting these reactions to our early efforts can give us insight into both our current relationship to our work and the possible conflicts and motivations of the adults who influenced us. These insights help us reclaim our power, and our art, for ourselves.

□ □ □

Exercise:

identifying your inner critic

Think back to the earliest creative effort you can remember sharing with an adult. Try to re-create your art: Write down as many words of the poem as you can reconstruct, draw the drawing again, sing or play the tune. As you do so, imagine that you are a child again and that this is happening for the first time. Feel the sunshine on your face as you sit in your childhood back yard, drawing; smell the pencil lead and your teacher's cologne; listen to the sound of the washing machine in the next room.

When you're sure you have recaptured as much of the experience as you can, open your notebook and write about it, quickly, without reflection. Capture as many details as you can. Try to answer these questions: How old were you? What spurred you to write, or draw, or compose that song? Did it spring from your own desire to express yourself, or was it a response to a suggestion or assignment? What were you trying to express, and what was your assessment of your effort? How do you feel about it, right at this moment?

Now switch the scene to where you show your work to an adult. Write down everything you remember about what the adult said—and everything that wasn't said but that you picked up anyway.

Look at your art again. Notice whether your response to your work has shifted based on what the adult said about it. How are you feeling about yourself, as an artist, right now?

Write down everything you can remember, everything you think about what you remember, and any feelings that come up. If any connections emerge between this scene and current feelings about your work, add those. Don't force anything, but don't skip any details because they seem stupid, trivial, or obvious. You aren't writing for anyone but yourself, and sometimes details that seem at first glance to be silly or irrelevant hold the key to deep feelings and important insights. Allow yourself to be surprised by what comes up.

During the next few days, pay attention to any other memories or insights that may surface. Write these down, too. When you feel you have learned everything you can from this exercise, add the pages to your "artistic autobiography" binder.

The point of this exercise is to spur you to consider what your early efforts, and the reactions of important others, may have meant to your development as an artist. The better we understand where we have come from, the more control we have over where we are headed next.

Bonnie, the photographer from Appalachia, declined to do this exercise at first. She told me, "There's no point in bothering with this. I know the answers. I was a regular kid on a loser path until a camera fell into my hands and I found my vocation. The first people who saw my pictures gave me a scholarship to study photography. A famous photographer discovered me, and my career was made. Clean and simple. Nothing before that affected me very much. My life began when I started taking pictures."

By that time, I knew that Bonnie had a way of blocking out inconvenient or uncomfortable experiences, and I sensed a conflict underlying her casual dismissal of the notion that anything of emotional import could have occurred before the contest that changed her life. I urged her to just try the exercise.

She made a cursory effort, a cartoonlike sketch of a cat on a porch railing. With a sardonic half smile, she added a white border to make the drawing look like a photograph. "This was the first picture I took," she said. "Everyone loved it. That made me happy. No surprises. Frankly, this is boring."

Sometimes, what is commonly known as "resistance"—refusal to engage in therapeutic exploration of an issue—can be a healthy and protective response. Pushing deeply into a trauma or intense conflict before we're ready can be harmful, and our psyches erect barriers to keep us from doing damage to ourselves. I thought Bonnie could benefit from this exercise, but I didn't want to force her into possibly dangerous territory. I knew from experience that if material needed to emerge, it would come up in response to gentle prompting when Bonnie was ready. So I dropped the subject and made a note to try again later.

As I'd suspected, Bonnie's flip statement, "No surprises," reflected a wish, not reality. She called the next day, sounding agitated, and asked for an extra session—"as soon as you can squeeze me in."

When I saw her that night, she started talking before she'd finished taking off her jacket. "It must have been the drawing that set it off," she said. "I was working in the darkroom this morning, and suddenly I was a little kid again, in my mother's kitchen.

"I used to love to draw. I drew all the time, everywhere. I hadn't exactly forgotten this, but I hadn't thought about it in years, either. Then today, it all came rushing back—the joy, and the feeling of rightness.

"I didn't imagine drawing as a career, or a ticket out of poverty, or anything other than what it was—a way to record the things I saw that nobody else seemed to see—or at least, they didn't see them the same way. Sometimes I'd draw pictures from my imagination, or cartoon characters or movie stars from the TV. Most often, though, I'd be mesmerized by something in our real life—an ant crawling on the windowsill, or my brother's shoe lying on the floor—and I'd go into a kind of drawing trance. I'd have to get it down on paper. I'd draw on old envelopes, paper napkins, even the wall once."

Bonnie told me that she didn't bother asking people what they thought of her drawings, simply because she didn't think of them as art or as achievements of any kind. Once they were finished, they were irrelevant—the pleasure was in the act itself. "So the electric bill would have pictures of my sister's ear on it, and the grocery list would be festooned with electrical wires," she recalled. "Everybody knew it was just something I did, the way my sister sucked her fingers and my brother liked to bounce balls. We didn't have art classes in school or anything; this was just something I'd picked up by myself."

One day when all of her brothers and sisters were roughhousing in the kitchen, someone knocked over a carton of milk. Bonnie described wanting to catch the scene in a drawing: "The milk seeping down the side of the stove—the two different kinds of white, and the way the drops pooled on the green linoleum floor—it was one of the most compelling sights I'd ever seen," she told me. "My mother yelled at me to right the milk and clean up the mess, but it was so beautiful—I couldn't do it. I said, 'Just a minute,' and ran off in search of something to draw with.

"My mother went ballistic. When I came back with a napkin and a pen and started trying to draw the milk, she ripped the napkin out of my hands and threw it away. Then she started hitting me everywhere—on my head, my back, my stomach, all over. She'd never done that before—a swat on the bottom, or sometimes if we really gave her lip, a slap in the face—but she never lost control, never tried to hurt us.

"She screamed at me that she was sick to death of my 'stupid doodles.' She said it was embarrassing having them everywhere, that people thought I was crazy or retarded because I was always drawing instead of talking right and doing useful work, that I wasn't a baby anymore and it was time I started acting normal. She forbade me to ever do 'that nonsense' again.

"I just stopped after that. I believed what she said—that the drawings proved I was stupid and abnormal. I thought this was something everyone had been keeping from me, the horrible truth. I didn't even have to try hard to break the habit; every time I'd find myself reaching for a pen, I'd feel a little sick. I guess I still noticed the same things, but it was lonely and sad to look at them and not be part of them by getting them down on paper. So after a while I stopped looking so much."

Bonnie, like many children, had taken her mother's angry words as gospel truth. I asked her to reimagine the scene from her mother's point of view. Bonnie told me, "We were really poor, and my mother worked hard for that milk. We had two main rules in our home: Don't waste food, and don't disobey. And here I was, breaking both. Of course she was angry."

I asked Bonnie whether she thought her mother really believed her drawings were a sign of a mental or emotional problem. She thought for a while and then said, "I did have an uncle who was slow, and everyone made fun of him. Maybe she was afraid it was hereditary. But looking back, I think she probably wanted to take the words back, but she couldn't. The way we were brought up, adults were supposed to be infallible. They never apologized or admitted they were wrong—to do that would be to lose authority. And in our household, she was the only parent. She was outnumbered, you know? If she'd started backing down in front of us kids, she'd have lost control."

That session marked a turning point in our work together. "I honestly didn't believe there was anything in my childhood to look at," Bonnie said. "And if there was, I didn't want to know about it—I didn't want to dredge up old dirt. I just wanted to come in here and fix my problems in the present, without all that navel-gazing. I guess I didn't want to be angry at Momma for taking away something I loved. So I just blocked out all that hurt. And that's what I keep doing, pretending that things don't matter when they do." Bonnie now tries to be more open to exploring underlying issues. She's learning that revisiting painful episodes won't kill her—and acknowledging anger at her loved ones won't kill them, either. She understands now that the point of looking at the past isn't "navel-gazing" or "dredging up dirt," but rather understanding herself so that she can function better in the present.

Bonnie has started drawing again—very tentatively, and she doesn't stay with it for more than a half hour at a time, because the feelings that surface threaten to overpower her. But she is glad to have reconnected with her love of drawing. She realizes now that her mother's characterization of her drawing as "crazy" and "retarded" was the result of anger and frustration, possibly mixed with ignorance. It wasn't a judgment about the worth of Bonnie's art, and it didn't have to keep her from doing what she loved. Like her photography, Bonnie's drawing is becoming a source of fascination and self-expression—one that she is determined never to give up again.

Bonnie has shown great courage in reexamining her childhood. She's not alone in her reluctance to revisit unhappy episodes, especially those that bring up unresolved anger and resentment against those we love. As difficult as that is, it can be even harder to turn the searchlight on ourselves and to look honestly at our own dark sides, as I'll ask you to do in the next chapter. The experience can be a rich and important one, though. As Bonnie said recently, "One thing I've learned is that you don't get to the treasure without wading through the muck."

art is
not always
pretty

embracing the

shadow self

Chapter Four

*i*n the previous chapters, we examined the messages we received about our identities as artists from our families, our communities, and the culture at large. This can be difficult work, because it entails acknowledging that trusted adults in our lives were far from perfect. It takes courage to revisit our childhoods, to relive painful experiences, and to challenge idealized memories. The rewards, though, are usually self-evident: We gain valuable insight into the impact of our early experiences on our development, and, by looking at our caregivers through adult eyes, we can often achieve a level of understanding, compassion, and forgiveness that is profoundly healing.

It's tempting to stop at this step. Many people want to, because at this point we tend to feel great about ourselves. We think we finally understand why we haven't produced the work we're capable of. We can forgive our loved ones and stop blaming ourselves. We're convinced that therapy is magic and that our therapist is a genius.

Unfortunately, insight and emotional healing, as important as they are, are seldom sufficient to get us unstuck. If we stop here, our focus remains external. We attribute our failure to excel to our parents, our teachers, and our cultures. This is a great way to let ourselves off the hook, but in itself, it doesn't move us forward.

The next step—the subject matter of this chapter—is the place where treatment often bogs down, and where clients start forgetting appointments and fantasizing about the spectacular vacations they could be taking if they weren't spending so much on therapy. This is where things get ugly—where I ask you to look at the least attractive, rational, and socially acceptable parts of yourself and to embrace them. This may be the single hardest task in therapy—and, for artists, the one with the greatest payoff.

The person whose story best exemplifies this process to me was not a client. She wasn't even an artist. She was a fellow participant in a workshop I attended on the treatment of eating disorders. "Jenny" was an attractive, average-sized woman who told me she used to weigh more than three hundred pounds.

Jenny's parents were part of a religious community that took the Seven Deadly Sins with great seriousness, particularly Gluttony and Lust. She said she'd been made to feel wrong and greedy for wanting food that was more plentiful and appetizing than the meager, dreary fare her mother served.

Jenny's family also believed that hugs and caresses led to impure, lustful thoughts, so she was seldom held as a child. She was ashamed of her longing for physical contact and, later, sex. When she sprouted hips and breasts as a teen, she interpreted these as evidence of her sinful nature and tried to starve her body into submission—but she would develop seemingly uncontrollable cravings for cookies and candy, which she would buy after school and gobble down before she reached home. By the time she was sixteen, she was obese.

As an adult, Jenny broke with her family and repudiated their religious beliefs. She entered therapy, where she gained valuable understanding of the destructive effects of her childhood messages, and she thought she had freed herself from them—but she stayed fat. Her pattern was to starve herself, ignoring her normal hunger pangs, and then find herself in front of the freezer having devoured a half gallon of ice cream, only half aware of what she was doing. She tried every diet and weight loss program she could find, but she couldn't break the pattern. She avoided looking at herself in mirrors and in the shower. She was shocked when she accidentally caught sight of her reflection as she passed a shop window or a department store mirror. Then she would quickly put the image out of her mind. She also ignored other bodily sensations, such as heat, cold, and the discomfort of sitting or standing for too long. In essence, she continually told her body it was worthy of contempt. And she kept eating and growing heavier, despite her desperate efforts to rein herself in.

This continued until she was in her mid-thirties, when an acquaintance made a chance remark that changed her life forever. What he said was, "You can't lose what you don't own." Jenny suddenly realized that she had never truly owned her body or its desires.

It was excruciating for Jenny to really look at her body and to acknowledge how large she had become, but she took this brave step. She practiced looking at herself in a full-length mirror and saying, "You're beautiful. I love you," even when she wanted to turn away in shame. It was hard for her to admit that she felt hunger and that she loved to eat, but she made herself stay in her body while she ate nourishing, appetizing meals. Once she started paying attention to her hunger, she began recognizing when she was full. She started to allow herself other physical pleasures, too—rubbing lotion into her dry skin, putting on a sweater when she was cold. She began to inhabit her body fully for the first time that she could remember. When she did, the weight began to come off, without dieting or deprivation.

I see this phenomenon frequently in my practice and in my own life. We sincerely want to make certain changes, whether it's losing weight or finishing our novel. We try, hard and repeatedly. We work to understand what's blocking us and try again, without success. And then, one day, seemingly out of the blue, everything shifts.

Of course, our new perspective doesn't just descend on us from on high. We have earned it with our previous work. This is why it's important when reading this book to do the exercises in order—one insight, one seemingly minor advance, prepares us for the next step, until, almost without realizing it, we are poised to take a leap that would have been unthinkable only weeks—or days—earlier. Only then are we ready to truly attend to wisdom we previously might have ignored or given only lip service to.

Often, that wisdom entails embracing the very quality we

have been trying so hard to get rid of. Like Jenny, we need to learn to love the parts of ourselves we were brought up to despise and eventually to banish from our awareness because acknowledging them would be too shameful. These parts, taken together, form what Jungian psychologists call the "shadow self." We believe, or try to believe, that if we don't acknowledge our shadow self, it will go away. But when we ignore and deny the qualities that don't fit into our idealized picture of ourselves, or that don't conform to the expectations of our family or society, this shadow self takes on a life of its own, sabotaging our conscious efforts to carry on with the life we believe we should be leading.

Jenny's story is a useful illustration of this principle because her weight was a dramatic, visible manifestation of her shadow self. The harder she tried to make it go away by ignoring her body and its signals, the more insistent it became.

For a blocked artist, of course, the struggle tends to be internal. To the outside world—and even to ourselves—we may seem to be functioning well. The fact that others can't see our conflicts so easily saves us some embarrassment, but it also makes our shadow selves easier to ignore. This was true in my case.

To all appearances, I had a fulfilling, even enviable, life. I performed well at a series of increasingly responsible and lucrative jobs and then made the decision to return to graduate school to pursue a career of service to others. I volunteered for causes I believed in. I had good friends and a strong marriage. On paper, this looks like a fine life, and I believed it was. When stirrings of dissatisfaction surfaced—hints that another, deeper life, and a more complicated self, lurked below—I pushed them down. Why rock the boat? Besides, with all of the real problems in the world—war, hunger, violent crime—what right did I have to be unhappy, to want something more for myself? I had plenty—to admit that it wasn't enough seemed shockingly, frighteningly selfish and greedy.

My dismissal of these inner promptings was fairly typical of the women I see in my practice. Because we are taught early on that pleasing and helping others defines our worth, the terms "selfishness" and "greed" tend to work on us the way Kryptonite affects Superman. They weaken our resolve and turn our brains to mush. We go through all sorts of contortions to avoid them, including denying our own needs and desires. Yet selfishness in its most basic sense—valuing the self and insisting on the validity of one's thoughts and emotions, however ugly or irrational they may seem—is fundamental to the creation of original art.

Male artists also struggle with their shadow selves, of course. For them—and for many women who buck the tide and pursue their art in the face of all opposition—the shadow self tends to be their softer, more vulnerable side, which many consider shamefully weak. Detachment from this "feminine" self can cut people off from important relationships and sources of nurturance. Lisette, the composer, split off her longings for friendship and love, fearing that any vulnerability to others would divert her from her work. Lisette, like my male clients, paid a high price for her single-minded devotion to her art—but she consistently created compositions of originality and depth. Unlike Lisette, most women who consult me can't even envision embracing the qualities that are necessary for producing art—tolerance for chaos; willingness to explore the depths rather than skate on the surface; and indulgence of the conviction that our time, thoughts, and feelings are important enough to override others' desires and expectations.

Maria, the Nuyorican writer, was haunted by the specter of selfishness as she tried to find the time, energy, and concentration to write while caring for her baby single-handedly. Maria is unusually forthright and self-aware, and, on a conscious level, she understood and accepted the conflict between her daughter's needs and her own. She said, sensibly, "Melissa's needs have to come first. If she's hungry, or her diaper needs changing, I can't expect her to suffer while I finish a thought. Even if she's just bored, I can't ignore that, because she can't pick up a book and entertain herself while she waits for me. I'm an adult; I should be able to deal with not getting everything I want."

Maria's rational, caring evaluation of her situation was, of course, accurate and realistic. But it also reflected what she thought she should say and feel. At first when I asked her whether she ever became angry about having to put her work on the back burner, she denied this energetically, saying, "How could I be angry at a little baby? I chose to have her; she didn't ask to be born!"

During the course of therapy, as Maria grew more comfortable exploring her less acceptable impulses—and as she grew to trust that I would not judge her for articulating them—a more complex picture emerged. Maria unearthed deep wells of anger at her husband, who felt entitled to relax and watch TV after a hard day at the office, since his work supported the family financially. She also resented her mother, who helped Maria's sister with childcare but left Maria to fend for herself. And, finally, after a long period of struggling with herself, Maria acknowledged that a part of her was furious at Melissa herself. "She's a vampire," Maria said. "She sucks all my blood. There's nothing left of me, and yet she always wants more. Sometimes when she won't stop screaming I want to throw her out the window."

These feelings terrified Maria, and not just because they represented a part of herself that she'd rather not identify with. Like many women, she was afraid that if she brought them to the surface and owned them, they would take over her personality, causing her to act out in antisocial ways. Maria felt she needed to disown her shadow self to keep from harming her baby.

The fear that acknowledging our shadows will turn us into monsters makes emotional sense, but in practice, the opposite is true. As Jenny's story demonstrates, it is the feelings we disown that become most problematic. Like unsupervised children, they run wild, scribbling on the walls, destroying the furniture, while the adult, our "nice," conscious self, sits primly reading in the next room. Taking ownership of these impulses gives us more power over them, allowing us to choose whether, and when, to act on them. And because we are imaginative, creative people, we are blessed with the ability to live out experiences vicariously through our art that would be unthinkable in real life. Maria discovered this shortly after the session in which she described Melissa as a vampire. A few weeks later she brought in a story that she said had "written itself," about a woman who is seduced by a vampire at a Halloween party and later gives birth to a baby who sucks her blood along with her breast milk. Her family interprets her pleas for help as symptoms of postpartum psychosis and has her hospitalized. The baby, made to drink bloodless formula, bites the family dog and cat, turning them into vampires as well, and baby and pets join forces to terrorize the remaining family members.

The story is a delight—funny, scary, and emotionally resonant, reflecting not just Maria's anger but, in its depiction of the baby's rage over being fed formula instead of blood, her comprehension of the danger of cutting ourselves off from the sources of our creativity. It offers a wonderful example of the treasures we can mine from the realm of our shadow selves. Too often, though, we are too frightened of our selfish, gluttonous, sloppy, lustful impulses to take advantage of this richness. We shove them underground, cutting ourselves off from all that makes us unique, from the source of our inspiration—and our work grows static and empty, if we can produce art at all.

My early work definitely suffered from the "nice girl" syndrome. From my teens until my late twenties—when I gave up entirely—I would periodically try to write a story, a poem, or, once, a play. My work wasn't bad, exactly. It was thoughtful, intelligent, and well expressed. Often, readers commented on the "elegance" of my writing style. That sounds positive, but the elegance was usually devoid of real feeling. It reflected what I thought a story or poem should be, not my true self—because I tended not to acknowledge that I had any feelings that would mark me as less than the kind, loving, tolerant person I needed to present to the world. Once in a while, my real feelings coincided with my beliefs about what I should be expressing, and the resulting work took on a life and authenticity that underlined the emptiness of my other efforts.

I hoped that therapy would help me to become a better writer. I was a great believer in therapy. Since high school, I had been fascinated by the study of human behavior in general, and especially psychodynamics—the idea that our unconscious desires and fears express themselves symbolically through our speech, behavior, and dreams. I read the basic works of Freud, Jung, and Melanie Klein long before I thought of going to graduate school in psychology. Yet in my own therapy, I got stuck in the "insight" phase, drawing meticulous lines between the childhood experiences I've described and the sparseness and shallowness of my work, but resisting any hint that there might be more to my personality than its compliant, reasonable surface. Eventually, I terminated therapy, believing I had gotten all the benefits it was capable of giving me—I had achieved important insights and my life was orderly and externally successful. It seemed I wasn't cut out to be a writer after all, but I was making a good adjustment. I was ready to move on, to become a psychologist, to dedicate my life to helping others heal. Like Cinderella's stepsisters, who cut off their toes and heels to fit into the glass slipper, I had cut off authentic parts of myself that didn't fit the cookie-cutter feminine ideal. My writing had suffered for this. My therapy patients would most likely have suffered, too, if it weren't for an incident that occurred in my second month of graduate school.

I was assigned to a field placement in the rehabilitation unit of a large, public, inner-city hospital in Brooklyn. Many of the patients I saw there were very disturbed, violent individuals; others were unlucky victims of hideous crimes, perpetrated by my criminal patients or by others like them. Hearing their stories— the anger and ruthlessness of the drug dealers and muggers, and the way the victims' lives were ripped apart—was profoundly disturbing to me. I had envisioned a career helping nice people who were depressed or anxious to overcome their inhibitions and resume normal functioning—not exploring the depths of human degradation and despair. I would often have nightmares on field placement nights.

One afternoon, I conducted a psychological interview, in an isolated office, with a man who revealed homicidal inclinations. He told me stories about people he had hurt and bragged that it was a point of honor to retaliate for any insult or slight with violence, even murder. He became increasingly agitated as he spoke to me. I asked him a question calculated to calm him down, and instead he reacted with anger. I was frightened for my life. By reminding myself of the advice of one of my teachers, that when a patient seems to be losing control it's vital to speak from your most rational part to his, I managed to persuade my patient to accompany me to the unit psychiatrist, who referred him to a closed psychiatric wing. Afterward, I was shaking so hard I could barely stand up. I went home thinking I might never return.

That night, though, I had one of the most memorable dreams of my life—one that is still vivid nearly twenty years later. I dreamed I was in a wooded area that, in the dream, was part of my graduate school. Other students and teachers were handling what looked like a toy dinosaur or dragon. One passed it to me, and as she did, I realized that it was alive and deadly. It leapt onto my shoulder and thrust its head toward mine. I woke up in a cold sweat with the certain knowledge that it was about to either kill me—or tell me the most important thing I had ever heard.

As I thought about the dream the next day, I realized that it was a message from my shadow self. The dinosaur/dragon symbolized rampant destructive powers but also vitality and ancient wisdom. I was at a crossroads: I could run away from the field placement, from the study of psychology, and from the requirement to delve into the dark side of the human psyche—my patients' and my own. I could continue to skim the surface of life and art. Or I could brave the depths, fearing annihilation but knowing that if I survived I would be immeasurably richer, deeper, and wiser.

Like Jenny, I experienced a seemingly instantaneous shift in perspective that was actually the result of years of incremental preparation. I was ready to dream that dream. I returned to my field placement and discovered areas of deep connection with even my most disturbed patients. I reentered therapy and committed to bringing all of my thoughts and feelings into treatment. It was a bumpy ride—much more so than my previous course of therapy had been—but I became a richer, more expressive person every day.

It took three more years—and the torture of being blocked on my dissertation—before I was ready to acknowledge my vocation as a writer. But I count that dream as the moment I made the commitment to embrace my shadow self, a commitment that allowed for the possibility of art and creativity to flourish in what had previously seemed arid and unwelcoming soil.

Normal socialization is enough to make many women disown their angry and violent impulses. Abuse can intensify these impulses in the victim, engendering conflict that can endanger not only their creativity but their very lives. This was Janna's experience.

"The whole time I was being abused," she told me, "and for quite a while afterward, I just shut down emotionally. I didn't want to feel the anger and shame, but it wasn't possible to turn those off selectively. If I let myself feel anything at all, the bad feelings would come rushing in. So I had to numb myself completely. I stopped laughing at jokes, I didn't enjoy food, I no longer read for fun or paid attention to movies or TV. I was a gray person living in a gray world. I did what I was told, and I didn't think any more than I had to. It wasn't exciting or fun, but it was the safest way I could see to exist in the world. I came to believe I didn't have emotions or even physical sensations. I could stick a fork in my arm and not feel the pain. Sometimes I would cut myself just to see myself bleed, to be sure I was alive."

As Janna approached adolescence, she began using drugs to numb herself. "Both of my parents kept samples of prescription painkillers in their offices. Just the word 'painkiller' made me feel a little calmer. It wasn't hard to figure out how to get into their cabinets, and I never took enough so they'd notice. I also started drinking at night to get to sleep. Sometimes I'd sneak into my father's liquor cabinet, and sometimes I'd give money to one of the homeless guys who hung out by the liquor store to go buy us each a bottle. I stole money from my parents to pay for it."

To an outside observer, Janna might have seemed well connected with her dark side—even to the point of having let it take over her personality. In fact, she was doing everything she could to keep her rage and shame from surfacing, even if it meant flirting with suicide.

For Janna, the conflict wasn't about presenting a "nice," sanitized persona to the world, and to herself, as it is for so many women. Janna's abuser had told her she was a dirty, depraved little girl, and she believed him—and the shame threatened to overwhelm her. In addition, like many abuse victims, Janna feared the murderous rage she felt toward her abuser and those who had failed to protect her—even her adored parents. Not only was she afraid her rage would explode and cause her to harm someone, she also identified her "evil thoughts," as she termed them, with Louis, her abuser. "Everyone agreed he was a monster who should have been given the electric chair. I thought so, too. But, guess what? I wanted to hurt him as badly as he'd hurt me—worse, in fact. I hated him so much I wanted to kill him. Sometimes I hated my parents, too, and the teachers who saw my sister and me going downhill and didn't even ask us about it—and the first therapist, who believed what Louis told her. Some days I wanted to kill them all. So, if Louis was a monster who didn't deserve to live, what did that make me?" To function with any sense of herself as a child who was entitled to love and care, Janna felt driven to split off and disown her "dirty, depraved" self, with its associated shame, along with her rage. She experienced this shadow self as so toxic and powerful that she needed drugs to keep it from contaminating the small sliver of self that still felt like a normal, lovable child.

Fortunately, before Janna's substance abuse and self-mutilation had caused lasting damage, the family's therapist guided her toward poetry and painting.

At first, it wasn't easy for Janna to express her shadow self through writing. "When I first started, every word felt like a lie," she said. "I'd write something very basic, like 'You betrayed me,' or 'I hate you,' and immediately I'd feel scared and ashamed. I'd think, *You know that's not true; what's wrong with you to say such a thing?* I had been telling my anger that it didn't exist for so long that expressing it felt alien and wrong to me. Besides, Louis always used to tell us what liars we were. I guess I'd bought it, even though consciously, by that time, I knew he was full of crap."

Nina, the therapist, wisely didn't push Janna to continue in an activity that caused her so much distress. Instead, she guided Janna toward painting.

"She set me up with tempera paints and huge rolls of brown paper and told me to just go at it. That was so freeing! I didn't have to justify my color choices or imagery; I didn't second-guess myself. I just threw my inner conflicts directly onto the paper. It wasn't art as I've come to define it—there was no plan, no conscious shaping—but it was real and direct, and it uncorked the feelings I'd bottled up and denied for so long."

In painting, Janna was able to express her shadow self for the first time. She still hadn't owned it, though, in the sense of acknowledging her shame and rage as valid parts of herself. Everyone's creative process works differently, but for Janna, the nonverbal nature of painting, which gave her the freedom to depict her feelings without explaining or justifying them, also allowed her to avoid identifying fully with them. "I needed to use language, to name my feelings, before I could really take them back in. That didn't come until I wrote that poem to my mother. That was when I said 'I'—'I hate you,' 'I hate him'—and when I described what Louis did to us, in detail. I wrote all of it out, and it was an assertion, a manifesto—this happened, this is how I feel, I'm no longer willing to deny or back away from it; deal with it.

"That wasn't art, either, of course. But like my paintings, it was the raw material of art. I needed to get it all out there, and to take it back into myself, before I could move forward with any kind of control. If I hadn't made those early paintings, I'd still be drawing cute little kittens. And if I'd stayed at the level of those paintings and poems, I'd just be vomiting out my raw emotions. That might be therapeutic, but it's not what I want. The challenge is to take the rawness, the unfaked reality, and make it say what I want to say, make it communicate in a controlled way. It's as if I have to feed the angry red paint splotches to the cute little kittens, to make them grow into leopards. Which means a merging of my reasonable, compliant self and my angry, raging bitch—the challenge of a lifetime."

Janna offers a graphic and emotionally accurate image of the task of the artist in integrating the shadow self. As conscientious adults, we need to maintain control over both our behavior and our material. But if we disown our anger, our vulnerability, our selfishness—whatever aspects of ourselves we feel we can't accept—we deaden ourselves to our deepest feelings, and our art, however formally flawless it may be, becomes forced and anemic. Exploring and embracing the shadow self takes courage, and shaping the messages it gives us into art demands discipline, commitment, and practice. But if our ambition is to create the most honest, original, emotionally authentic art we are capable of—and of course this is your ambition; if your intentions were frivolous you wouldn't have read this far—the value of this work is immeasurable.

Exercise:

communicating with your shadow self

Imagine a day without consequences. You can do or say anything you like, and you can refuse to do anything you don't want to do. Nobody will remember any of this tomorrow. In fact, it won't have happened. You can eat whatever you want without gaining an ounce, you can conduct an affair free of guilt or complications, you can even commit murder—and your victim will spring back to life tomorrow.

What would you choose to do? Write down what such a self-centered, uncensored day would consist of.

Start with waking up: What would you have for breakfast? Crêpes suzette? Pizza? Scotch? Would you share your meal with someone special or eat it in blessed solitude? What would you do next? Fly to Paris? Crash Oprah's show and tell the world your life story? Lie in bed eating chocolate and watching old movies?

Take yourself through the day, imagining and recording every indulgence.

How would you characterize a person who behaved the way you would on your No Consequences
Day? What might she look like? Imagine such a person. Draw her picture. Give her a name.

Then talk to her, in the privacy of your mind. Tell
her it's safe for her to show herself, that you will neither punish her nor act on her dangerous impulses.
Ask her how she feels about your life, and what she
wants from you. Write down her answers.

Consider this the beginning of a dialogue with
your shadow.

When I asked Elizabeth, the eighty-two-year-old novelist, to try
this exercise, she was skeptical. She told me, "I dealt with all of
that shadow stuff back in the '70s, in my consciousness-raising
group. I went in afraid of ranting, hairy-legged feminists—afraid
that I would turn out to be one, of course—and came out with a
much more integrated sense of myself as a woman. It changed my
writing enormously."

From what Elizabeth told me, it sounded as though she
had done important work on her shadow self. I asked her to try
the exercise anyway to see if anything new came up. She said,
"The day I would design for myself is exactly like my actual life.
My book and movie deals have made me quite comfortable, and
there's really nothing I want to do that's beyond my means."

Elizabeth is both adventurous and cooperative, and it wasn't like her to resist an exercise. I asked her to walk me through her day, even if it seemed silly.

She described her favorite breakfast, an asparagus omelet and black coffee on her deck, and then said, "I know what! Instead of my morning walk I'll go for a jog. That will be a real consequence-free day—no shortness of breath and no osteoporosis!" She told me about a wooded area behind her house and said, "I'll start there."

It seemed that Elizabeth's fantasy day was going to turn out to be as pretty and orderly as her actual life. Then she said, "There's a path I've never seen before—maybe I should follow it." I encouraged her to take it wherever it led her. We were both surprised when she said, "I'm at Margaret's!"

Margaret was her ex-husband's mother, an upper-class snob who had never accepted Elizabeth. Elizabeth had always treated Margaret with courtesy and respect, and Margaret had responded with dismissive rudeness and snide references to Elizabeth's working-class background. "Go inside the house," I instructed her. "What do you see?"

"I'm in the kitchen. Margaret is cubing ham for a soufflé. She's explaining how to make it, as though I couldn't possibly have ever seen one before."

"How do you want to respond? Remember, this is your free pass to say or do whatever you like."

Elizabeth started to answer me. Then she stopped dead. Her face was pale. "What just happened?" I asked her.

"I picked up a kitchen knife and stabbed her."

Elizabeth was shocked at the degree of rage she harbored for a woman who, as she said, had been dead for forty years. I was surprised, too, that her shadow had emerged so quickly and dramatically. However, Elizabeth had had years of therapy, consciousness-raising groups, and other awareness-enhancing experiences by the time she began seeing me—and she also tended to work in an accelerated fashion, feeling, as she said, that there was little time to lose.

I reminded her that this was just an exercise, and that she really hadn't killed anyone. "I know," she said, "but that felt so real—so right."

Like Maria, and like many of my clients, Elizabeth was afraid that the emergence of her shadow self signaled murderous impulses that she was liable to act out in real life. As a novelist, she was well aware of the boundary between imagination and reality, but the depth and intensity of her impulse to kill her mother-in-law shook her to her core. "I knew I disliked Margaret," she told me, "but hate her? She wasn't that bad! Besides, I don't believe in hate."

Our feelings, though, exist whether we believe in them or not. And as we talked, Elizabeth recalled numerous instances when she had swallowed Margaret's verbal abuse. "Did you ever think about answering back?" I asked her.

"Not really. Richard was her only son, and I was an outsider to their circle. She felt I'd stolen him away from her. Mostly, I wanted to reassure her, to blend in to the family so she wouldn't resent me so much. And I didn't want anger and fighting to be part of my new life. I'd had enough of that at home, with my father getting drunk and beating us kids, and my brothers always scrapping over something. I wanted to shape my life, and my husband's and children's, into a work of art."

Clearly, though Elizabeth had told herself that her response to Margaret should be tolerant and understanding, her shadow felt differently. I asked her to give this other, hateful self a name. She thought for a moment and then said, "Biddy. That's what my family called me. I started using Elizabeth because Margaret refused to say the name 'Biddy.' It was too low class to pass her lips."

I asked "Biddy" what she thought of Elizabeth, and she immediately answered, "She's 100 percent fake. A plastic doll. Boring." Asked what she wanted Elizabeth to do or say, she replied, "Tell the truth for once. Stop being so goddamned perfect. Get her hands dirty."

When we concluded the exercise, Elizabeth reported feeling shaken but intrigued. She asked me, "Do you think I'm fake and plastic?"

Elizabeth was definitely not plastic. She was, and is, warm and genuine, and I told her so. But giving voice to "Biddy" had shed light on a part of her personality that warranted further exploration. We discussed Elizabeth's childhood love for books that depicted beauty and harmony, in contrast to her shabby and often violent home life. "Biddy," it seemed, represented the parts of herself that Elizabeth had felt she needed to dissociate from, first to emulate the heroines of her beloved books, and then to fit into Richard's more refined world. Was it possible, I asked her, that Biddy had anything important to contribute to her life or work?

"She's an ignorant, resentful, impulsive harridan," Elizabeth told me. "I can't see how I would benefit from knowing her." But a few minutes later, she added, "I wish I'd had the guts to keep my own name, though."

We talked about the significance of taking both a new first and last name when she married. "I felt as if I were wiping the old me out, erasing her and starting new. It was what I wanted to do. I'd always felt my family wanted me to stay down there in the scrap heap with them, and my life depended on escaping. And then, there was the failure of my novel, which I also wanted to leave behind. So my marriage was a chance to move into the gracious circles I'd always aspired to. I guess I felt that Elizabeth could belong in that world, but Biddy never could."

But Margaret made it clear that Elizabeth didn't belong there, either. "Biddy would have fought back, I guess, but I'd given Biddy up. Elizabeth was a lady, and ladies were kind and gracious. They didn't speak disrespectfully to their mothers-in-law."

I asked her whether she thought Margaret had been a lady. She was nonplussed. After a long pause, she said, "Margaret was no more a lady than my mother was, or than Biddy." Then she laughed. "Biddy would have seen that, wouldn't she? I wonder what else she saw that went right over my head."

Reviewers and readers frequently refer to Elizabeth as "a modern Jane Austen." She had always claimed to be flattered by the comparison. She said now, though, "I think that's what Biddy meant by 'plastic.' I love Jane Austen, but there was only one Jane Austen. When people are always comparing you to someone else, that means you're not writing like yourself, or not entirely. I wanted to be part of Richard's orderly, beautiful world and to create order and beauty in my books. It's still what I want. But maybe it's not what Biddy wants. And maybe Biddy is the real writer—the one who has something real and original to say."

I am a fan of Elizabeth's writing. It is not "fake" or "plastic" in any way. It is subtle, clever, and nuanced. I don't think she was as cut off from her authentic self as this episode seems to suggest. I also don't think "Biddy" really wanted to kill Margaret—I believe that Elizabeth's shadow wanted to free her from her thrall to Margaret's world and to encourage her to value and explore her own.

And Elizabeth is doing this. She has begun a new book. It doesn't sound like a dramatic departure from the rest of her work—it is set in the upper-middle-class suburban environment that she has made her own, and it concerns a marriage that is triangulated by a jealous mother-in-law. Elizabeth reports, though, that she feels new power in her portrayal of the daughter-in-law. "She's an interloper from a crass, blue-collar family. She doesn't know beans about baking a soufflé, and she doesn't care about learning. She throws the heirloom china in the dishwasher and feeds the baby straight from the jar. And she's not the villain, she's the heroine!"

This exercise can be hard to begin. Often, we resist challenges to our self-image, and we may be afraid of what lurks under the surface. But it is only when we acknowledge our hidden needs and desires and truly listen to what our shadow selves have to tell us that we can begin to function in an integrated, wholehearted way. As Rilke said, "Perhaps everything terrible is in its deepest being something helpless that wants help from us."

the impossible position

managing

motherhood and

creativity

Chapter Five

finding the time and energy to create art is problematic for many women who aren't parents. Few of us can support ourselves through our art, so usually we juggle jobs and other obligations that consume our creative resources—and it's hard for many of us to feel justified in carving out space for "selfish" pursuits. When children enter the picture, the conflict between external demands and the pull of our inner lives can intensify and threaten to overwhelm us.

As a therapist and the mother of an active twelve-year-old, I struggle with conflicting demands and desires every day. Many days, I think I must be crazy to have imagined I could do all this and write, too.

Recently, for example, a well-known novelist approached me to contribute to an anthology. Because I'm interested in the topic and enjoy her work, I really wanted to be a part of this project. The deadline was tight, though, and I was already overbooked. The last thing I wanted was to say yes and then fail to come through. Looking at my calendar, I realized that I had a few scattered hours during the coming week, followed by an entire Monday to myself—no clients were scheduled; my son, Ben, would be at day camp; and my husband, Bill, would be at work. Bill offered to take over all kid-waking, breakfast, and nagging duties on Monday to give me uninterrupted writing time.

Since I knew what I wanted to write about, I decided I could pull this off. I agreed to turn the essay in by Tuesday.

I awoke at five-thirty Monday morning and poured a cup of superstrong coffee, ready for a twelve-hour writing marathon. I pulled out the notes I'd scrawled during the week and settled in. An hour later, I was lost in the essay when Ben stumbled out into the living room. "I have a stomachache," he said.

My second thought was, *Poor kid. He's having such a rough summer.*

My first thought was, *Oh, crap.*

This, for me, is the paradox of parenthood. Ben inspires me. He wrenches my heart open, forcing me to become both stronger and more vulnerable. In trying to comprehend his development, I stretch and grow myself—in empathy, in understanding, and in the willingness to face down my own demons so as not to visit them on him. As I become a better, stronger, realer parent, my writing deepens and grows more courageous and authentic.

At the same time, parenthood frustrates and sometimes exhausts me. I don't have enough hours in the day, and when I do get a moment to myself, a never-ending to-do list tends to be attached to it. Even when I think I've budgeted my time accurately, I always face the chance of a monkey wrench, such as Ben's illness.

My anthology essay worked out. Ben wasn't sick enough to require a visit to the doctor. He rested, we read and talked, and then he played a computer game while I bulldozed through the rest of the essay. It wasn't the finest piece of writing I've ever produced, but it was good enough. The editor suggested some revisions that strengthened it, and I was in. Like most mothers, I've had to give up my ideal of creating perfection in order to get anything done at all.

And I'm one of the lucky ones: I have a supportive husband. I have had several artist clients who were single parents, who reported feeling tired and distracted all the time. Other artist-mothers are in relationships, but their partners leave most of the organizational or grunt work to them—and they are burdened with resentment along with the added work. And nearly all of us struggle with guilt about snatching time away from our kids to nourish our own dreams.

I realized that I needed to reclaim my identity as a writer when my inability to progress on my dissertation forced me to confront the ambitions I had cast aside long ago. But I didn't actually complete my first serious story until Ben was three. And motherhood has played a huge role in my continuing metamor-phosis from inhibited people-pleaser to committed artist.

I've described how I was trained to swallow my authentic responses when they didn't conform to the prevailing ideal of how nice girls should feel or behave. Even after I became aware of this pattern—and its inhibiting effect on my writing—I didn't recognize how ingrained it was. This was, in some ways, because my life was too easy.

Before I had Ben, I tended to socialize only with people like me—pleasant, literate adults, with tastes and values similar to mine. It's not that I don't have strong, controversial opinions—I am a feminist, prochoice, pacifist Quaker. I've arrived at my beliefs through serious soul-searching, and I don't shy away from expressing them. In the past, though, this didn't require great courage, because I surrounded myself with people who thought as I did. We bolstered each other's ideas and attitudes rather than challenging them; we went out of our way to treat our minor differences with tact and discretion. Once, a friend's husband made a blatantly racist remark at a party I gave. I stared at him and said, "I'm sure you didn't mean that." When he didn't back down, the conversation simply resumed around him, and no one addressed him for the rest of the evening. After that, I made sure to see my friend without her husband. That was as confrontational as my friends and I tended to get.

In the workplace, too, I was insulated against controversy. Like many professionals, I've chosen to work in offices and agencies that reflect my core beliefs. I've certainly had to deal with difficult clients, coworkers, and supervisors, but they haven't been the norm, and when I think I've been pushed too far I've always had the luxury of knowing there were plenty of jobs in my field. Once, when a supervisor who had become increasingly hard to work with reprimanded me for a messy desk and a run in my pantyhose—at the end of a twelve-hour workday—I simply smiled, agreed to do better, and put the word out that I was looking for a new job. I found one within the week.

Skating on the surface this way—never being forced to

delve too deeply into anger or controversy—makes for a comfortable existence, but authentic art is seldom generated from the comfort zone.

Motherhood has changed all that.

In the first place, Ben himself pushes every button I've got. Simply by being a kid—losing the expensive winter jacket he's had for just a week, continuing to play a computer game after I've reminded him repeatedly to start his homework, or debating the justice of a household rule or punishment with such relentless vigor and persistence my head starts buzzing—he taps into wells of irrational anger no problematic supervisor or dinner guest could ever approach. And for the first time, I can't smile and walk away, even if I wanted to—which I don't. I can't grit my teeth and deny my feelings, either, because he *sees* me—he'll say, "Stop yelling at me!" and if I insist that I'm not yelling, that I'm just speaking firmly—he's not buying it. He knows yelling when he hears it, and, unlike my friends, he has no intention of supporting my illusion that all of my reactions are attractive and nice. His honest, unmediated responses force me to confront and examine my own in a way I've never had to do before, not even in therapy. I don't always like what I find, but the process of owning my less attractive attributes has resulted in grittier, more substantial writing that I probably would never have achieved on my own.

Loving Ben puts me in other situations I can't walk away from, either. For example, he has played on Little League teams with kids whose parents are worlds away from us politically. We spend every baseball season in close proximity to the other team parents, and when the conversation turns to party politics or social issues, I need to decide whether to risk offending them or to swallow my real feelings for the sake of "niceness" and superficial peace. Because I know Ben looks to me as a model for navigating the social world, I'm increasingly likely to opt for defending my beliefs as diplomatically as possible. This takes more courage than I would have imagined back when I was cocooned. It's hard for me to invite argument, to take the risk that people will be angry at me or dislike me. Often, asserting myself is accompanied by an emotional reaction—my hands or legs shake, or my eyes fill—that makes it clear to me that there is a deeper significance to what I'm doing. What's happening is that each time I raise my voice, no matter how tentatively or awkwardly, I am reclaiming a part of myself that I had thought I'd lost. And the more risks I take, the more comfortable I become with others' disapproval—and that's reflected in my writing, too.

Finally, there is the issue of my response to the people who hurt Ben—other kids who, being kids, sometimes snub him or ridicule him; the coach who cuts him from the team; the teacher who punishes him unfairly. What I have to push down at those times isn't a nice girl's desire to be liked; it's a mother bear's instinct to kill anyone who threatens her cub. I have never felt such visceral hatred for any human being as I do for the ordinary, basically decent folks who have made him cry. The experience of such strong, nearly overpowering feelings has broadened my understanding of people who actually are overpowered by rage and commit unthinkable acts—and the requirement to channel these feelings into words that will help the situation, not actions that will worsen it, presents technical challenges that translate into enhanced verbal expressiveness and fluidity.

Understanding that true creativity entails discovering, acknowledging, and embracing the "shadow self" is one thing. Doing the work—and finding the courage to express what I've discovered—is a never-ending struggle. When I grow complacent and lag behind, Ben is there pushing me forward.

More and more, I am writing from my heart, not from an idea of what will "sell" or what people want to hear. Moreover, engaging with his quirky intelligence as it develops has expanded my own understanding of creativity and given me permission to "play" in ways I've never allowed myself.

And, ironically, now that I'm in touch with so much richness and nerve, I can barely find the time to write a grocery list, much less an essay.

Before Ben was born, I led a fairly orderly professional life. I took it for granted that I would make my deadlines and complete my projects—that this was how conscientious people conducted their lives. Of course there were emergencies, but for the most part I worked around them. I finished my master's thesis propped on pillows in front of the computer with a killer throat infection and 102° fever. I studied for a psychology final in the veterinarian's waiting room, soothing my terrified, cancer-riddled cat with one hand and turning pages with the other, straining to decipher the words through my tears. I crammed for another exam huddled in a friend's broken-down car, waiting for the tow truck. Real, non-negotiable crises, such as my father's death, were rare enough that I felt entitled to ask for hiatuses and extensions in my work, and I was confident of receiving them without being penalized.

All of that is in the past. I have missed important meetings because of a runny nose that disqualified Ben from preschool. I was once called out of an intense session with a client by a frantic baby sitter who, unable to find the bottles of breast milk I had pumped, was helpless to comfort my screaming baby. And I've shown up badly prepared and bleary-eyed for important presentations, workshops, and interviews after staying up all night as he suffered through an ear infection or a terrifying dream.

And, again, I'm one of the lucky ones. Many women, such as Maria, struggle with partners who discount their needs and devalue their commitment to their work.

Maria is married to a busy attorney. When she first started therapy, she was so exhausted and depressed I was afraid she might be suicidal. She was left alone with her one-year-old daughter, Melissa, all day and well into the evening. Her husband, Jim, thought that because of his demanding job, he should not have to help out around the house. Even though he made decent money, he balked at the idea of hiring a baby sitter so Maria could write or even rest. He claimed that his own mother had raised three children and kept their suburban house spotless, all without help, and he couldn't imagine why Maria couldn't manage with just one small baby.

"Jim is always annoyed with me because the apartment is a mess and there's never anything to eat," she told me. "I'm so tired that sometimes I forget to shop, or I'll forget there's a pot on the stove until it's burned past saving."

When I asked about her writing, she said, "Sometimes, if Melissa is playing quietly, or napping, I'll run to the computer and try to work on a story, but if Jim is home he'll make some remark about the dirty dishes or the empty refrigerator. I can't think straight anyway, so nothing I write makes sense.

"I don't know how his mother did it, or how anyone does this. I see other mothers in the park, with two or three kids, and they look so rested and happy. The kids are immaculate, and the moms are in great shape and stylishly dressed. They always have these little containers of cereal, and boxes of wipes, and they're perfectly organized and on top of things. They don't even talk to Melissa and me, and why should they? I'm a fat slob with spit-up on her shirt and a diaper bag that looks more like a garbage pail. My family always said I was a screwup and a loser, and I've never felt it so strongly."

Maria had fallen into a trap many mothers are prey to: judging her performance as a parent by the (probably imaginary) standard set by others. Whatever Jim remembered, it is unlikely that his mother raised three children and managed a household with no help at all. Probably a housekeeper was in the picture, or a parent or sibling who lived nearby, or perhaps she exchanged childcare with neighbors. I reminded Maria that she didn't know the life stories of the "perfect" park mothers, either. Maybe they have nannies at home, or maybe they can pull it together to get to the park but their homes look like disaster zones.

Even if these other mothers really were perfect housekeepers, that didn't mean Maria was a "screwup." I asked her whether there were any aspects of mothering that she enjoyed and felt competent at. She said, "I love singing and playing with Melissa. She's already talking a bit, and we do little songs with hand movements together. She likes looking at picture books, too. She'll point to an illustration and I'll tell her what the object is called. Lately, I point to them and she tells me! It's so exciting, watching her learn new things every day."

I pointed out that having a mother who read and played with her was probably more important to Melissa's development than a spotless house or an organized diaper bag. That sounds obvious, but so often we take our strengths for granted and exaggerate our shortcomings. It's important to focus on what we're doing right—especially if those around us are quick to point out where we fall short.

After we had worked together for several weeks, I suggested that Jim come to one of our sessions. I don't do couples therapy, but if a client's issues are intertwined with a partner's behavior, it's sometimes helpful to hear the partner's perspective and assess strategies that might be useful.

Jim agreed to come, which was a good sign. We met on a Saturday, because he was unable to get time off from work. He arrived looking as haggard and miserable as Maria. Melissa examined the room as we talked, running back and forth to point out items of interest to her mother. She was a cute, extremely energetic little girl and it was clear that both parents adored her.

"Melissa never sleeps for more than a few hours at a time," Jim told me. "Maria can catch up on her rest during the day, but I have to go in to work exhausted, and I'm making dangerous mistakes. Maria doesn't understand how stressful my job is or what our life would be like if I lost it. Then, after a grueling day, I come home to a pigsty and I have to forage for my own dinner."

It was clear that both Maria and Jim felt stretched to the limit of their resources. What also seemed apparent, though, was that Jim was making some unsupported assumptions. He had stated implicitly both that his work was more demanding than caring for a child, and that, though he understood Maria's situation, she could never understand the pressure he was under or the real-life consequences of failure.

Maria had told me from the first session that her family thought of her as a child because her gifts were more creative than practical. It seemed that Jim had absorbed the same attitude.

I asked Jim to tell me what had drawn him to Maria initially. He smiled and said, "She was the most original, alive person I'd ever met. She looked at the world in a completely different way. And her stories were amazing. We met in a writing class where we were supposed to be peers, but she was a pro and I was a rank amateur. I was bowled over from day one."

Asked the same question, Maria told me, "I was attracted to Jim right away—who wouldn't be? Plus, he was the first person I'd ever met who was competent in the world and also really got what writing was about. I loved his stories—they were very different from mine, very spare and logical, but he lived them out in his head, the same way I did. I could talk to him as an artist and he didn't think I was crazy. Now he does, just like everyone else."

The cliché "opposites attract" has its basis in the common human tendency to be drawn to people whose strengths complement ours and compensate for our weaknesses. We admire others who are skilled in areas we haven't mastered, and of course life is easier when one partner can take over the tax returns while the other nurtures the couple's social life.

Once we're in an established relationship, though, we tend to punish our partners for the very attributes that drew us to them. What we once saw as fascinating originality we now experience as frustrating immaturity, and practicality translates into unimaginative plodding.

This is an issue for many couples, but in my experience, it's more intense for women artists, especially when a child enters the picture. Artists of both genders are often seen as childlike, impractical dreamers with limited ability to cope in the "real world" of commerce and competition. Traditionally, in our culture, women who care for children are seen in a similar light, as less smart, competent, and worldly.

Anyone who, like Maria, has toiled at an unrewarding day job to support her art, or who has managed to keep a small child safe, healthy, and nourished for any extended period, is living proof of the fallacy of this stereotype. Our primary focus may not be on getting ahead or balancing the books, but most artists and mothers are forced to develop at least rudimentary life skills (and many, of course, are highly accomplished professionals and businesspeople). It's also arguable whether emotional connectedness, physical nurturing, and daily responsibility for the survival of another human being are less important contributions to the "real world" than making money. But the impression persists, in part, I think, because "women's work" is assumed to be inherently less important and difficult than the tasks traditionally assigned to men, and in part because money is a widely accepted marker of success and status in our culture, and labors of love such as art and parenting are seldom financially profitable.

Even in relationships that begin as equal, mutually admiring partnerships, as Maria and Jim's did, the balance often shifts when a child enters the picture. No matter how liberated we believe we are from traditional gender roles, they tend to exert a strong pull on new parents. Parenthood is an exciting, but often terrifying, venture into unknown territory, and when we're feeling insecure and stressed, we seek certainty and stability, even embracing roles we may have consciously rejected. In addition, for many families, the presence of a baby evokes powerful, often unconscious, childhood memories—including recollections not just of our own family dynamics, but those of favorite books, films, and television shows—accompanied by a desire to re-create for our own children the sense of warmth and safety they gave us.

As we talked, it became clear that both Maria and Jim had fallen prey to this common phenomenon. Faced with the responsibility of supporting his new family, and with a desire to give Melissa the best of everything, Jim had concentrated his already practical focus on making and saving money, as his father had done. He was haunted by the idea that he could fail at his job and let Maria and Melissa down. Maria's tentative suggestions that they hire a cleaning service or baby sitter to give her some relief panicked him—and he was outraged by what he saw as selfishness and irresponsibility in her desire to spend money they might need for Melissa's future.

Jim had found joy and fulfillment in creative writing in college, but he had shelved his own creative ambitions in favor of more practical pursuits. From what I could see, Jim had split off his vulnerable, artistic side because he had gotten the message from his own childhood that this was his duty as an adult—and we have seen what happens to the parts of ourselves that are rejected and denied. Pushing down his artistic yearnings made him resent Maria's continued commitment to her writing. He experienced her desire to carve out space to write not as a valid expression of her vocation or a need to preserve the identity that was being subsumed by motherhood, but as shocking immaturity and self-indulgence.

Maria, for her part, had bought into the idea that childcare and homemaking were her province alone, regardless of her own talents and inclinations. She didn't question the assumption that her failure to perform up to the standard set by Jim's mother—despite their very different personalities and gifts—was evidence that she was a "screwup." Jim's attitude toward her perceived deficiencies echoed her family's, causing her to feel that he was right. "I guess I can fool people for a while into thinking I'm okay," she said. "I even fool myself. But in the end, I just don't have what it takes. Things that come easily to normal people defeat me."

Child rearing doesn't come "easily" to anyone, though some people find the practical aspects more manageable than others, and the expectation that women should conform to some cookie-cutter homemaking ideal is unfair. We don't expect all men to be skilled accountants or construction workers; why should women have to be great housecleaners, cooks, and diaper-changers simply because they are mothers? But this expectation is reinforced everywhere we turn.

As a mother of older children said, "Even though I work outside the home, 90 percent of the 'invisible' childcare tasks fall to me, seemingly by unspoken universal agreement. If one of my kids gets sick at school, I'm the one who's called. I'm in charge of scheduling dentist and doctor appointments and making sure the kids keep them—and if there's a cavity or an iron deficiency, nobody lectures my husband about too much candy or the importance of spinach. My youngest boy has learning disabilities and some behavior problems, and every time he fails a test or gets into a fight at school, guess who's supposed to drop everything and run over to meet with the teacher? To add insult to injury, sometimes the housework or laundry piles up because of work deadlines or a sick child—and everyone feels sorry for my husband, being married to such a slob."

The expectations and cultural biases against mothers and artists, taken together, can create a burden that feels overwhelming. It's not right that we are expected to carry more than our share of domestic responsibility, to squeeze our diverse skills and interests into a narrowly defined role, or to endure devaluation of our life's work as a disposable frill or selfish indulgence. But feeling misunderstood and denigrated is historically part of an artist's life and identity, and cultural presumptions—and even the unrealistic demands of our own partners and families—don't have to prevent us from pursuing our art.

What does hold us back is our own capitulation to these expectations. It takes enormous strength to buck the cultural tide and our personal conditioning, and rejecting a partner's claims on our time and attention, no matter how unreasonable, can feel cruel. There is also a shift in power when a woman stays home with her children or takes a less-demanding job to be available to them, even in the most enlightened and egalitarian relationship. No matter how supportive or trustworthy our partner is, we're aware of our financial vulnerability, and we feel pulled to defer to the breadwinner's wishes.

This was Maria's situation. After I had met with Jim and reassured myself that he wasn't trying to undermine or hurt Maria, her treatment goals became clearer. We concentrated, first, on communicating to him the necessity for some kind of household help to enable Maria to catch up on her sleep. He had been moved, in our joint session, by recollections of the "old Maria"—the joyful, creative, spontaneous partner he had been drawn to and cherished. Once he was reminded of those early days, he was pained by the contrast with her current state of exhaustion and despair. In therapy, Maria and I role-played conversations in which she reminded him that she was not his mother, in many positive ways as well as the obvious negative ones, and that chaining her to the kitchen wouldn't make her a good housekeeper any more than forcing him to practice scales would turn him into a concert pianist. Jim was able to hear this and agreed to pay for both a weekly cleaning service and a teenage baby sitter to help out after school so Maria could nap.

Once Maria was feeling less sleep deprived, her depression lifted and our work progressed more rapidly. She was able to think more clearly and could use her limited writing time efficiently. She wasn't producing at her earlier rate, but even finishing a story every month or two helped her reclaim and sustain her identity as an artist—and this had an enormous positive effect on both her marriage and her self-esteem. She began chatting with other mothers in the playground, and she discovered that she wasn't alone in her feelings of inadequacy and exhaustion. She now trades baby-sitting services with two congenial neighborhood mothers. She watches all three children one morning a week, buying herself additional writing time. She has started participating in readings again, bringing Melissa, who has become an unofficial mascot in her reading circles. With her encouragement, Jim has started writing again, too, and he's more supportive of her efforts now that he's allowing himself his own creative expression.

Even though it's vitally important to insist on our identities as artists in the face of others' attempts to define us, it's just as critical not to judge ourselves if we simply can't keep up with our children's needs and churn out the Great American Novel or a symphonic masterpiece while they nap. Some of us have exhausting jobs that don't allow for a lot of flexibility or free time. Some of us are single parents or have ill or disabled children whose pressing, immediate needs take priority over our own. If taking time for ourselves would cause our children real hardship, then of course we have to make sacrifices—not because we're women, but because we are responsible adults.

Even in the most difficult situations, though, it's usually possible to carve out time for self-expression if we truly believe we're entitled to it. We can trade childcare with others, as Maria does, or seek out programs that offer relief to the parents of children with special needs. And we can lower our expectations for housework, cooking, and all the nonessential chores that our children don't really care about anyway, to concentrate on what's important—their health and happiness and our art. We may also need to set smaller, more achievable goals for ourselves for a while—a story or poem instead of a novel, pencil sketches rather than oil paintings, a song in place of a symphony. What's crucial is to keep the light burning.

We can pursue our work despite social pressure, time constraints, and our own conditioning only if we ourselves believe it is important enough to sacrifice perfection in other areas for. We can't wait for someone else to give us permission to call ourselves artists or offer to watch the kids while we work—it has to come from us. And as we discover and build our own strengths while helping our children to nurture theirs, we often discover that "impossible" tasks are within our grasp after all.

Exercise:

claiming creative time (for mothers only)

Find a quiet place at a time when you are unlikely to be interrupted. Have someone else watch your child. If necessary, fake a doctor's appointment for a mysterious ailment to guilt a friend, relative, or neighbor into babysitting.

Now use the time you would have spent on an exercise actually making art.

Repeat as often as necessary.

damned
if we do

the perils

of artistic

success

Chapter Six

many women artists who consult me have already experienced some success. They have created work that is considered promising or has even achieved renown. They have been immersed in their art, excited by it, dedicated to it—and now, for reasons they can't explain, it has all ground to a halt.

Some are in the throes of debilitating creative blocks. They are either completely unable to work, or are producing work so slowly, or so far below their standards, that they find it unbearable. They have missed deadlines. They have put on twenty pounds through repeated, frustrated raids on the refrigerator brought about by staring at a blank screen. They are addicted to the Internet. Some have turned to alcohol, drugs, or ill-advised sexual entanglements as distractions from their inability to work.

Others consult me because, although they are working well, they are screwing up in other areas of their professional lives. They may accidentally erase important phone messages from agents or gallery owners, lose entire chapters in a computer crash because they forgot to back up their manuscripts, or show up drunk to performances or showings of their work.

For all of these women, the initial interview, whether on the phone or in person, tends to be emotionally charged; often it's hard for me to understand what a woman is saying because her words are so choked with tears. This is partly because of the very human tendency to put off getting help until things have reached the crisis stage—when a career is veering toward the rocks or a secondary problem, such as alcoholism or an extramarital affair, has gotten out of hand, bringing with it desperation and shame. For many women, though, the most frightening and disturbing aspect of the situation isn't its effects—the professional setbacks or personal complications, as difficult as these can be—but its perceived cause. As Maria, the short story writer, said in our initial interview, "If I had a stroke and couldn't use words, it would be horrible, but I'd deal with it. I'd go on with my life somehow. But knowing I'm doing this to myself—that I'm sabotaging my best efforts, that I can't trust myself to be on my own side—makes me feel crazy."

Freud believed that while self-defeating behavior in men indicated an inner conflict that required treatment, the same behavior in women was normal—and even expected. His explanation was that women are naturally masochistic: We enjoy being in a one-down position and will do whatever is necessary, consciously or unconsciously, to ensure that we stay there. This is because, on some level, we are aware that we are inferior to men, biologically, intellectually, and morally, so self-sabotage ensures the preservation of the natural order.

Freud was a brilliant theorist and writer, but his gift for recognizing and analyzing unconscious motives did not extend to his own misogyny. The notion that women are oppressed because we want to be—because we even, on some level, enjoy being thwarted in our ambitions—is a convenient one. It serves to perpetuate a system that favors men, while letting individual men off the hook. After all, if we are engineering our own career suicide, and deriving satisfaction from it, there is no need to change anything, right? There is nothing to take responsibility for, or feel guilty about, because we're all happy with the way things are. (When I discussed this idea with Lisette, the composer, she commented, "Just like abolition was unnecessary because the darkies were so happy on the plantation.") I believe the expediency of this explanation for our failure to achieve explains, at least in part, the pervasiveness of the belief that women don't want to succeed in the same ways men do, long after Freud's biological interpretation has been discredited. Nowadays, of course, we don't talk about penis envy or female masochism. Instead, we call it "fear of success."

This isn't to say that women don't engage in stunning acts of vocational sabotage. Of course they do. Artists of both genders shoot themselves in the foot at alarming rates, and in my experience women really are more prone to undermining their careers than men are. But the reasons for any person's apparent self-destructive behavior are complex, and to write this phenomenon off in women as "fear of success" is to blame the victim. (When men stop producing or flame out in other ways, their actions are often interpreted as manifestations of profound artistic torment or a response to the indifference of the commercial world to the pure-minded artist. While these explanations are equally simplistic, they at least lend dignity to a tragic struggle and can even spark public interest in the artist's work.)

So why do otherwise intelligent, gifted women derail their life's work, often at the moment when they are about to break through into a deeper level of self-expression or reach a wider audience?

The issues we've explored in previous chapters—especially negative messages from our families and communities, the scarcity of appropriate role models, and failure to address the shadow self—are usually part of the picture. But these factors alone don't explain why women who seem to have it all together suddenly derail.

With both men and women, I start by exploring the content of the stalled project. Sometimes the subject matter of a novel or painting evokes disturbing feelings or unresolved conflicts. Elizabeth, the novelist, for example, once found herself unable to continue work on a book she had been excited about. When we went over the novel's plot in detail, she realized that a minor character's miscarriage had triggered sadness over her own miscarriage, which occurred as her marriage was breaking up. Her feelings of loss had been subsumed by her distress over her husband's affair and their divorce, and she hadn't realized how much the episode still affected her. Elizabeth chose to address her grief in therapy and resume work on the novel. Other clients decide to move on to another project and deal with the associated feelings at another time. Either way, the block is usually limited to the work at hand and is dissolved quickly.

When the problem is more global, we need to look at the client's beliefs about the consequences of success. Every client's story is different, but I have found that many women harbor unconscious fears of exposure or of hurting a loved one—or, in some cases, both.

□ □ □

Even after women have removed many obstacles to creativity and are producing authentic art, we often falter at the next stage—when our work begins to garner attention and especially when we are faced with the task of promoting it.

It isn't easy for anyone who creates serious art to bring it to the public's attention. When we write, or paint, or compose from places deep within ourselves, putting our work out to be judged by an unknown audience can be unsettling, even threatening. And self-promotion is even more complicated for women, who have often internalized cultural prohibitions against "pushiness."

These conflicts are fairly easy to bring to the surface, though. What is often overlooked is the deep-seated fear many of us harbor about being looked at.

The first time Maria came to see me, she exhibited symptoms of depression and crippling insecurity. She told me that the prospect of submitting her stories for publication brought up fears that journal editors would laugh at her pretensions to being a writer. She became so agitated before reading her work to an audience that she would throw up before going onstage, and she gave me a laundry list of reasons why she would be bound to fail at publicizing her book if she ever finished it: She was too fat, she was not photogenic, and she stuttered when she was nervous.

Maria's writing was stalled primarily because she was too exhausted to think. Her low self-esteem made it hard for her to take her needs seriously, including the need for relief from twenty-four-hour childcare, and it caused her to devalue her highly original, imaginative stories. During the course of our work together, her confidence grew, and she started feeling entitled to the time and space she needed for her work. Her daughter's growing ability to care for herself and, especially, to sleep through the night also helped Maria to reclaim her identity as an artist.

As Maria rededicated herself to her work, her writing became even more original, powerful, and rich. She took pride in her growing mastery of her art, and as she grew more accustomed to publication, her fear of being mocked for daring to think of herself as an artist diminished—yet it didn't go away, and she still became nauseated before readings. When she was invited to participate in a televised reading to benefit a women's shelter in the South Bronx, she agreed, because it was a cause she cared about. Then she developed a cluster of physical symptoms—a painful sore throat, diarrhea, and shortness of breath—that her doctor couldn't find a medical explanation for. Because all of these problems would interfere with her television appearance, we both suspected a connection.

Some writers simply aren't good performers. Their words

come alive on the page, but they don't relate well to a live audience. Forcing themselves to perform is self-defeating; they need to find other ways, such as a website or an Internet blog tour, to make their work known. I didn't think this was Maria's problem, though. In our sessions, she was articulate, engaging, and funny. Despite her stage fright, she was in demand as a reader, and the producer of the shelter benefit had invited her to participate after watching her at a spoken-word event. But every time she made a public appearance, she said, "I feel as if I'm going before a firing squad."

When I asked her to imagine the worst possible outcome of the TV show, she said, "I go on and everything about me is wrong. I have a huge stain on my blouse and nobody tells me. I look fat and ugly. I lose my place in the story and the audience gets bored and impatient. I start stuttering. Nobody can understand a word I'm saying. I let everyone down."

I pointed out that the show's producers had an investment in its success, and it was unlikely that she'd be allowed to go on camera with a "huge stain" on her clothing. In fact, because the show was to be taped, any major gaffes could be edited out, and if her performance were truly hopeless, it would simply be cut. "They'll make sure you're dazzling," I said, trying to ease her anxiety by teasing her a bit.

After a pause, Maria said, "This is going to sound crazy, but that would be even worse."

I listen especially closely when clients preface a statement that way. Usually, thoughts that seem "crazy" to us don't even make it into consciousness, and when they do, we dismiss them. A thought that is powerful enough to break through our internal censors usually represents an important truth demanding expression.

I asked Maria to elaborate. "Don't worry about not making sense," I said. "Just say what comes to mind."

She told me that when I'd said the word "dazzling," she had an image of herself in a low-cut, sparkly red dress, with her hair upswept, giving a confident, flawless performance.

"What's the feeling that goes with that image?" I asked.

"Terror."

"You're terrified of . . . ?"

"Rape," she said, surprising herself.

Maria had never been sexually assaulted, she told me, but this was a constant concern in the crime-ridden Bronx neighborhood where she grew up. Her family was protective of Maria and her sister, Cecilia, and the girls were not allowed out at night without a male relative. "When we did go out, we got all kinds of warnings about what to wear so we didn't attract the wrong kind of attention. No short skirts, no high heels or red lipstick—we had to look like ladies," she told me. "Somehow, that was supposed to protect us from predators.

"There were girls in the neighborhood who dressed in a sexy way—skimpy spandex outfits, lots of makeup. When my grandmother saw them, she'd spit and call them *putanas*—whores. The implication was that they were 'asking for it'—that if they were assaulted they'd have nobody to blame but themselves."

Despite Maria's conservative dress, her appearance drew catcalls on the street because of her large breasts. "That frightened me," she told me. "It was just talk—nobody ever touched me—but the threat was always there."

Even worse than the fear, though, was her shame. "I felt like it was my fault—like, if I was a good girl, they would respect me and leave me alone. Since they were treating me this way, I must be a *putana,* too. I must be asking for it."

Maria now lived in an upscale community, and the neighborhood where her parents still lived was gentrifying rapidly. Street crime was no longer a constant worry, and Maria had not connected her performance anxiety to her earlier experiences. "I thought it was about being too ugly," she said, "but it was really about being too attractive—in the wrong way."

"What would the right way be?" I asked her.

She again surprised herself by blurting out, "There is no right way. If they look at me, they want to hurt me, and it's my fault."

Maria's feelings of shame and fear are not unique. Even in environments that are considered safer, we learn that nearly everything about us is subject to comment and criticism. When I was a teenager, unattached boys would often congregate at the entrance to a school dance and loudly rate the girls' appearances on a scale of one to ten. We used to make jokes about the "meat market" to steel ourselves for this ordeal—but the humiliation we all felt as the objects of this kind of evaluation was no joke. I had thought we'd become more civilized since then, but my younger clients tell me the scrutiny has just moved to new locales. They describe feeling self-conscious at the gym, where a woman in workout gear using the machines will attract groups of men (often with beer bellies themselves) to gawk and comment on her shape. They tell me of feeling humiliated when photographs and videos of other women—actresses who may have posed in the nude before becoming famous, public figures caught in unflattering clothing and hairstyles, and ordinary women with vindictive coworkers or ex-boyfriends—are posted on the Internet to be dissected and discussed in crude terms by scores of anonymous commenters with macho-sounding usernames.

Janna, the painter who was sexually abused as a child, works as a word processor in a large Manhattan law firm. Several months ago, she alerted me to a discussion board aimed at law students that was circulating around her firm. The student association at one of the member law schools had decided to raise funds by producing and selling a "cheesecake calendar" featuring photographs of nude female law students. When one student tried to organize a protest, labeling the project sexist and demeaning, her photograph was posted on the discussion board, accompanied by speculation that her objections were fueled by jealousy because such a "fat pig" would obviously never be chosen for the calendar. Some posters described their fantasies of performing violent and degrading sexual acts on her without her consent.

Janna brought this material into our session because the violent imagery sparked flashbacks of her childhood abuse.

"What makes it worse," she said, "is that so many of the guys in the firm don't get it. They would never talk that way about a woman themselves, but they can't understand why this student lodged a formal complaint with the administration. They think she's making a big deal out of nothing—that the people posting the messages are immature jerks, and she's overreacting—she should just shrug it off and get a life. They think the whole 'psychodrama' is pretty funny. Reactions like that trivialize women's fears and make it harder for us to feel safe anywhere."

It's often hard for men to understand how frightening and intimidating this kind of attention can be. A man's appearance is not usually used as a weapon to discredit his ideas, and men, at least those who don't present as flamboyantly "effeminate," are not routinely threatened with sexual violence. But women don't need to have lived through Janna's ordeal of sexual abuse or Maria's verbal harassment to understand, on a visceral level, the implied threat to those who assert themselves or get out of line, or even who, like Maria, have looks that draw attention.

If it were possible to shift attention from our looks to our work, most women artists would choose that option. But women who don't look particularly "sexy" or attractive get noticed and criticized for that, too. In fact, there is no way to draw attention to our work without attracting notice to ourselves. Men have widely accepted "uniforms" for various roles—business suits, dinner jackets, "casual office wear"—and a limited range of hairstyles and accessories that allow them to blend in if they want to. The ability to downplay their appearance enables them to keep the focus of attention on their work, their conversation, or the agenda at hand. Women have no such options. As Janna said, "All the men in my office wear a dark suit, a light shirt, and a tie, so when they talk about a work issue, that's what registers—not their clothes or the color of their lipstick. If I wore an outfit like that every day, people would think I was making some kind of militant statement. But if I wear lace or bright colors, people always say something—even if it's something as innocuous as 'nice dress,' it's clear they're looking me over. And makeup! If I don't wear it, I look 'dykey,' and that's considered bad. But if I wear too much, I look like a slut, supposedly, and that's bad, too. I hear them talking about other women that way. And don't even get me started on shoes!"

Janna's paintings often deal with the sexuality of young girls in thought-provoking, disturbing ways. She has noted that male viewers and gallery owners assume an overly familiar, suggestive tone with her when talking about the sexual elements in her paintings, as though they are unable to differentiate the subject matter from the creator. "This doesn't happen so much with male artists," she told me, "even the ones who make really graphic art, with explicit sex or violence. If someone gets to be famous, his private life might be of interest, but the real focus is always on the work."

She attributes at least part of this confusion to the lack of "protective coloring" for women and finds it inhibits her ability to promote her paintings. "Part of selling artwork is being in the 'gallery crowd,' talking up the right people," she told me. "When the gallery owners or potential buyers are men, which they often are, there's always the problem of what I'm communicating through my clothing and my attitude. If I look sexy, if I'm too familiar, will they want to sleep with me as part of the deal? Will they assume I want to sleep with them? But if I'm distant or drab, there's no engagement, and that carries over into how they see my work."

When Maria and I explored her feelings of shame at being so visible, she was taken aback by the realization that she had been blaming herself for a situation that not only wasn't her fault, but that there was no way to escape. "No matter what I do, I'm different from men—and since men are considered the norm, women can't help being seen as abnormal," she said. "It's like when you read a book—you assume the characters are white unless the author tells you otherwise. Then they're black characters, or Hispanic or Asian characters—they're never just characters. They're never just people."

Janna's years of therapy to deal with her abuse have sensitized her to issues involving sex and power. Because she is aware of the complications involved in promoting her work, she is able to make conscious decisions about how to handle them. For example, she has accumulated a wardrobe of "gallery clothes"— tailored pants and stylish, but not revealing, sweaters that she has chosen for the relaxed yet professional image she wishes to communicate. She has perfected a cordial but distant manner to use with people she doesn't know well. She has become skilled at deflecting personal conversation back to her work. "It's hard," she says. "I'm actually a very emotional, spontaneous person, and I'm most comfortable flopping around in sweats. I feel like an actress wearing a costume at these events. But if I don't have the option of blending in, I need to manage my image carefully, to keep my work, not my appearance, in the forefront."

Other women, such as Maria, whose experiences are less dramatic and overt than Janna's, have to work to understand their reluctance to put themselves forward. They often feel, as Maria put it, that they are "crazy" and self-defeating. Usually, though, when they do make the connection between their "crazy" behavior and the beliefs that fuel it, it is possible to find ways to deal with their fears. Once Maria realized that her dread of performing wasn't really about being ugly or giving an embarrassing reading, she could acknowledge that she is actually a good performer who enjoys being in front of the audience. She noted that her panic always occurred before a reading; during the event itself she was fine. "As soon as I walk out, I'm in the present—I see the actual people in the audience, who aren't a bunch of street hooligans and don't want to hurt me—and I start to relax." To prepare for the TV show, we created a visualization exercise in which she envisioned a friendly, supportive crew and a benign audience. Maria practiced this two or three times a day until the filming. Her symptoms disappeared, and the show went off smoothly. We adapt the visualization exercise to accommodate each new engagement, and she's doing well.

Not all fear of exposure has to do with sexual threat. Some

women report being humiliated by other girls, especially in adolescence; others remember a teacher shaming them in front of the whole class. Whatever the original issue is, though, the problem is usually exacerbated by the woman's awareness that her appearance and presentation can't escape scrutiny, that she can't blend in. Recognizing the impact of our visibility can give us the tools we need to protect and reassure ourselves and go on with our work.

□ □ □

As we have seen in earlier chapters, many women are conditioned to put others' needs first. Many of us also grow up feeling that our self-worth depends on the success of our relationships. If a woman believes that getting ahead in her career threatens or harms a loved one, she may hold herself back from achieving all that she is capable of.

The person she is protecting may not have asked her to sacrifice herself this way and may not be aware that she is doing it. In fact, I have worked with both men and women who have discovered that the source of their failure to progress in their careers lies in the fear of outstripping a long-dead parent. Sometimes, as Janna discovered when she did the exercise at the end of this chapter, we turn this principle on its head and unconsciously hold ourselves back to punish someone who would benefit from our success.

Most often, though, when a woman inadvertently sacrifices career opportunities, the object and beneficiary is her romantic partner.

Bonnie, the photographer, first came to see me because she was failing to fulfill professional obligations, in a way that jeopardized her career. A major gallery owner had offered her a one-person show, and an art-book publisher was interested in putting out an accompanying volume of her work. "It's the chance of a lifetime," she told me, "and I'm blowing it right and left. I'm forgetting appointments, sending material to the wrong person, losing prints and even negatives. Not only that, but I'm afraid I'm getting a reputation as a flake, and nobody's going to want to hire me anymore."

Like Maria and many other artists who seem to be working against themselves, she worried about her mental stability. "You'd think I was possessed," she told me. "I have always been a capable, responsible person, and now there's this other person who's taken over and is determined to screw up. Every time I start to go through my files or return phone messages, I get distracted. I remember that I need to call my sister, who has been ill, or transfer money to cover a check. Then my concentration is lost, and I forget what I sat down to do."

After gathering her history (which you have read about in previous chapters), I asked her to describe what was going on in her current life. She told me she was in a ten-year relationship with a wonderful man, a fellow photographer, and that he was very loving and supportive. She was concerned about him, though, because he had health problems and hadn't been taking care of himself lately.

This information raised a red flag. Her partner's decline in health and self-care could be completely unrelated to Bonnie's situation, but the fact that they coincided with her "chance of a lifetime" might not be an accident. I pressed her for more details.

Bonnie told me that when they first met, she was thirty-one and Steve was forty-three. After more than a decade of working as an archivist at a news magazine and selling her photographs on a freelance basis, Bonnie had just been hired by a magazine as a staff photographer. Steve was well known in the field, particularly for his photographs for this magazine, and Bonnie had admired him from afar since her teen years, when she had first seen his work. "He was a romantic figure," she told me. "He was famous for his willingness to put himself in dangerous situations, to do anything it took to get the picture. He'd been everywhere and knew everyone. He'd published a book of photographs from the Bosnian war; they were tragic and haunting. The book won a major prize."

Bonnie's father had abandoned her family when she was four. Her mentor, Frank, served as a surrogate father to her in many ways, but Frank had children of his own, and though he was very fond of Bonnie, his primary interest in her was professional. I think Bonnie still hungered for personal attention from an older man. Steve's accomplishments and charisma made him especially attractive to her.

Even though Bonnie is normally very shy, she loses her reticence when she is excited and inspired. The first time she met

Steve, she peppered him with questions about his photographs. He was happy to talk to such an intelligent admirer, and they soon began meeting for lunch. "Steve was the only person I knew, outside of Frank, who I could really talk to about the experience of taking pictures, of framing a shot, of catching just the right moment when the sun casts a certain shadow that makes everything look deep and important, and you know you've got it," she told me. "There's nothing like that! He was very patient with my questions and took a real interest in my own work, criticizing my pictures and giving me helpful pointers.

"He was also so kind about guiding me through the political maze at the magazine. He told me who to trust and who to avoid, and he was always right."

It wasn't long before Bonnie had developed a full-fledged crush on Steve. She didn't expect him to return her feelings. She still thought of herself as the frightened country girl whose shabby clothes, crooked teeth, and "hillbilly" accent made her the butt of jokes.

But Bonnie had changed since those days. Once she was earning decent money, she had her teeth straightened and began buying more professional, flattering clothes. Her accent had softened a bit, and many people found it unique and charming. Even though she still felt awkward and shy, she was now an attractive, interesting woman. It wasn't long before the friendship deepened into romance.

When Bonnie described the early days of their relationship,

she kept using words like "kind" and "patient" to describe Steve. That wasn't the impression I got from her stories, though. It sounded to me as though Steve was flattered by Bonnie's obvious crush and enjoyed her deference. When she talked about his kindness in guiding her through the office politics, I imagined that it made him feel powerful to choose Bonnie's friends and allies for her. It sounded as if he were "patient" with her questions about technique because he liked expounding on his ideas while she hung on his every word.

This isn't to say that Steve was a monster or a villain. He was clearly a brave, gifted artist who genuinely cared for Bonnie. But as a celebrated photographer, he was used to being the center of attention and the most successful person in the room. His relative status and his readiness to steer Bonnie's career set up a power differential from the beginning.

Creative women, even those who grow up in intact, supportive families, often report feeling "different" or "odd" compared to their peers. Their unique way of looking at the world can be hard to communicate to others, and often their seriousness and drive make more lighthearted or superficial people uneasy. As a result, many artists feel isolated and unattractive. They are so grateful for any romantic attention, especially from someone who seems socially adept, that sometimes they mistake exploitation for benevolent interest, and they fail to notice danger signals that are obvious to an outside observer. And talented women frequently enter into relationships with older, more established men who are less threatened by their ambition and accomplishments—at least until the women start surpassing them.

In Steve, Bonnie felt that she had found the love of her life. After a year in which they spent every moment together between assignments, Bonnie left her studio apartment and moved into Steve's loft. They talked about marriage but felt no need to rush into it because they had agreed not to have children. "I feel sad about that," she said. "I always assumed I would have kids. But Steve was right—with both of us bouncing around the world on assignments, it would have been nuts."

Again, Steve seemed to be calling the shots. Moving into Steve's loft was logical because it was larger and better appointed than Bonnie's studio, but it also meant that Bonnie was the newcomer in territory Steve had already established. And although many women make the positive, realistic choice to remain child-free, Bonnie's lingering sadness and her statement that "Steve was right" suggested to me that her "decision" might have been more of an accommodation—and that Steve's reluctance might reflect a disinclination to share the spotlight.

I've described this relationship in a way that makes it sound pathological, because these are the details that jumped out at me in our initial interview, when I was looking for clues to Bonnie's professional dysfunction. In fact, there is never a perfect balance of power in any relationship, and this one had many strengths to counterbalance its evident weaknesses. Steve and Bonnie shared a deep love of their art, a dedication to using their work to benefit humanity, and a commitment to one another. As long as Steve remained the more successful of the two, both partners were happy and fulfilled in the relationship.

But as Steve entered his fifties, the physical stamina that he counted on to keep him at the top of his profession began to deteriorate. He developed diabetes, and his frequent travel across time zones made it difficult for him to adhere to a strict diet or remember to take medication on time. He tried to keep his condition a secret in this competitive field, but he became tired more easily and it showed in his work. "He never missed a deadline, and even his worst pictures were competent and interesting, but he stopped taking so many risks—and art directors noticed," Bonnie told me. The best assignments started going to younger, more energetic photographers.

Bonnie tried to help Steve out by cooking nutritious meals and calling and emailing him when he was overseas to remind him to take his medicine, but he resisted her efforts. "He told me to stop acting like his mother," she told me. "So I backed off."

When Bonnie got the call about the gallery show, Steve was in Afghanistan. She immediately called him, and he congratulated her and told her he was excited for her. But when he returned home, he seemed depressed and angry. Bonnie attributed his attitude to the atrocities he had witnessed and documented in the war zone, as well as to his health problems, and she resolved to be patient and understanding even when his treatment of her bordered on abuse.

"He kept harping on how I'd gained weight while he was gone. In fact, I'd been putting on weight slowly over the past few years—I used to be really skinny, but my metabolism slowed down after I hit forty. It didn't happen all at once, but he hadn't noticed it before, or at least it hadn't bothered him. Now he started calling me 'Porky'—'affectionately,' of course, so I wasn't supposed to take offense. One night as we were settling down to watch the evening news, I put my feet into his lap, as I often did. He said, 'Get your big fat feet off of me.' I didn't know how to react."

Bonnie is a smart woman, and if she had heard this story about someone else, I have no doubt she would have made the connection between her gallery show and book deal and Steve's surly behavior. Like most of us, though, she resisted the knowledge that the person she loved and trusted was not entirely on her side.

I have never met Steve, so I'm just going on what Bonnie told me, but I believe he genuinely wanted to support her. He may even have been delighted about her exciting opportunities if they had come at a time when he was feeling better about himself. I think, though, that like many men, Steve was conditioned to believe that his self-worth depended on his professional standing. When Bonnie threatened to surpass him in their field, he reacted—probably unconsciously—by lashing out at her. He punished her in other ways, too—again, probably without meaning to.

"A few months ago, he quit taking care of himself," Bonnie said. "He isn't supposed to have alcohol, and he's always chafed at that. He's started drinking gin and tonics in front of the TV. Not just one or two, but until he passes out on the couch."

Bonnie agreed that Steve's health problems and behavior were distracting her from her work, but she insisted that he was wholeheartedly invested in her success, as she was in his. She wouldn't entertain the possibility that he could be conflicted about the shifting power balance in their relationship. And because she wouldn't let herself recognize his ambivalence, she also couldn't see the ways she protected the relationship by making sure she didn't get ahead of Steve.

Since we had just started working together, I didn't push Bonnie to accept my analysis. She had no reason to trust my judgment about her relationship, and I didn't want to scare her off. Instead, we focused on practical solutions to the immediate problem. Since she was able to accept the idea that the stress of dealing with Steve's health and behavior issues was impairing her ability to function, we started there. At my suggestion, she asked her mentor, Frank, to recommend a temporary assistant to help her get organized. He sent a bright and ambitious photography student who was glad to take over the detail work in exchange for a small stipend and the chance to work with Bonnie. We made lists of tasks she needed to accomplish, and Jeanette, the assistant, carried them out.

In the ensuing weeks, Bonnie's show started coming together with Jeanette's expert help, and Steve stepped up his unacknowledged campaign to undermine her. While on assignment in

Europe, he caused a car accident after a night of drinking and was arrested. The magazine pulled strings to get him released, but the editorial director made it clear that he would hesitate to hire Steve again. Bonnie thought she had protected her show against self-sabotage by hiring Jeanette—but now she began drinking, too, telling herself that she needed the occasional glass of wine to relax. When she nearly passed out over lunch with the gallery owner, she realized she was in crisis.

This time, when I raised the possibility of a connection between her success and Steve's issues, Bonnie was able to hear it. We had begun to form an alliance, and she knew I wasn't trying to turn her against Steve. She told me she was terrified of losing him—but she was equally afraid of losing her career. "I've worked all my life for this opportunity," she said. "I would never force Steve into a situation like this. I'm not about to let him drown, but I can't let him ruin my chances, either."

Bonnie confronted Steve about his behavior. This wasn't easy for her—she was in the habit of deferring to him and working around his moods, and she feared that if she stood up to him directly, he would either up the ante by becoming suicidal or throw her out. As she said, though, "If my failure is a condition of Steve's love, that's not real love, and I don't want it. If that's the case, it's better to know now. We can't go on the way things are."

Steve denied any competition with Bonnie—in fact, he told her it was ridiculous to imagine that her little show and book compared in any way to his award-filled career. But when she threatened to leave him unless he entered counseling with her—and he saw that she meant it—he reluctantly agreed.

They are seeing a skilled couples therapist now, and Bonnie reports that they are making progress. Because Bonnie had always believed that Steve held all the power in the relationship—she felt he was conferring an honor on her simply by allowing her to live with him—their therapy has been a revelation to her. Steve has uncovered many insecurities of his own, including a deep fear that Bonnie will leave him if he fails to live up to her romanticized image of him as a daring, invulnerable genius at the top of his game. They are working out newer, more equal ways to live together and support one another.

In the meantime, Bonnie and I continue to work on strengthening her self-esteem and addressing the other artistic issues described in this book. She no longer feels "possessed," and she has resumed control of her career. She told me recently, "I love Steve, and I always will. I have every hope that we'll stay together permanently. But I will never let him, or anyone, pull me off track like that again. I'd give my life for him if he needed it, but I won't sacrifice my career to his ego or anyone else's. I'm better than that."

Exercise:

dealing with fear of moving ahead

Sit in your quiet place with paper, a pen, and crayons or colored pencils. Think about your work and your ambitions. Imagine that you can be as successful as you want to be. What would that look like—your own gallery show? The number-one spot on the best-seller lists? Performance of your work by the New York Philharmonic? Let your imagination run wild until you see a vivid scene in your mind's eye.

It's sometimes hard for women to give themselves permission to imagine extravagant success. Remind yourself that this is just an exercise, and it doesn't have to be realistic. You can be as ambitious as you like. When I did this exercise, I imagined giving my acceptance speech for the Nobel Prize for Literature!

Whatever scene you settle on, visualize it as specifically and concretely as you can. Pay attention to the nonvisual aspects as well—the taste of the wine at the opening, the aroma of your morning coffee and the crackle of the newspaper as you open it to the best-seller list, the sounds the audience makes as it quiets down for the performance. It often helps to imagine your own appearance and sensations at the event—what clothes are you wearing? What does your perfume smell like? Are your shoes comfortable?

Once you have fixed on a vision, try to draw it— with your nondominant hand, if that doesn't produce a completely undecipherable mess. Put in as many details as you can.

Then, while looking at the picture, write down all of your thoughts about the scene, as quickly as possible (again, with your nondominant hand, if you can). Most likely, the positive associations will come first. Keep writing, changing hands if you need to, and see what else comes up. Don't suppress any thoughts because they seem silly or don't make sense—as we've seen, these are often the most important insights. Just keep going.

When you run dry, ask yourself the following questions, and write down the answers:

☐ Who is unhappy about my success?
☐ Who was I pleasing by my failure or lack of ambition? How does she or he feel now? How do I feel about it?

□ Who have I been punishing by not succeeding?

□ Who won't love me anymore?

□ Now that I'm successful, what's next?

Then complete the following sentence: "If everyone looks at me. . . ." Again, don't think about it—just write as many endings as come into your head.

Put the page away for a few days. Then, again in your quiet corner, go over the list and highlight any odd or surprising responses. Write down any new associations to these responses and any thoughts that occur to you.

Take it out again in a week or so. See if you can discern a pattern to your answers, especially the highlighted ones. Think about what this might mean. If your answers confuse you, talk them over with a trusted friend.

This exercise can bring to the forefront conflicts that we've been suppressing or avoiding. For example, even after we thought we had addressed all of the reasons for Maria's difficulty promoting her work, she surprised us both by her response to this exercise. She visualized winning the National Book Award and then found herself writing, "C. pissed." Following this thread, she realized that she had always been afraid to outdistance her older sister. "Cecilia was so protective of me, and she was always willing to play with me when we were kids, but it had to be by her rules, with her playing the teacher and me the student, or she was the mommy and I was the little girl. I realized that it's the same way now—she's the big accountant with the nice house and the perfect life, and I'm the loser little sister. She is good to me, but at a price. And maybe I hold myself back because I'm afraid to rock the boat.

"I don't even care that much about awards. I don't think they necessarily go to the best writers—in fact, singling someone out as 'the best' when you're talking about creative work is bizarre. But I would like my work to be taken seriously and read more widely, and maybe I have been putting the brakes on in ways I hadn't realized."

Janna imagined an installation in the Museum of Modern Art. "Everyone came—including my asshole stepfather, Louis. He walked in and put his arm around me and called me 'Sweetie,' the way he used to. He acted like it was all to his credit. He would always do that, when one of us got a good grade or positive attention for anything. It was like he owned us, so he owned anything we did. And I didn't want to give him that. In fact, in the imagined scene, I turned around and kicked him in the balls—right in the museum! Maybe I'd rather stay obscure my whole life, working in a law firm, than share a triumph with him or risk a scene like that."

To say that Bonnie, the photographer, suffers from "fear of success" is to oversimplify—she is afraid that professional success could damage or destroy her most cherished relationship. Maria struggles with old fears of sexual assault and the threatened loss of her sister's support. Janna fears a recurrence of invasion and boundary violations, as well as her own rage. Who wouldn't be afraid of those things? But they don't need to cripple us or hold us back. In fact, dealing with them can make us stronger women and more confident artists.

Often, simply identifying the root of a problem gives us insight into potential solutions. At other times, awareness on its own can't solve the problem. This is especially true when there are two people involved, as in Bonnie's case. You may need to talk the situation through with a trusted friend or counselor, or you may need to simply push yourself to keep going, slowly, paying attention to whether the feared situation materializes, and weighing its costs and benefits.

As we will see in the next chapter, the commercial aspects of the art world can discourage even the most secure and dedicated women. That is why it is so important to be sure we aren't working against ourselves as we move forward in our careers.

a
woman's
place

creating art

beyond what

is expected

Chapter Seven

the previous chapter dealt with the impossibility of "blending in," since a woman's appearance and behavior are often judged along with her work, while men don't face such concerns to nearly the same extent. But even when we can manage our personal appearance and presentation to keep the focus on our work, the work itself is still treated much differently from men's—even in this day and age. I experienced this firsthand when I was twenty-eight and wrote a one-act play.

I didn't set out to write a play—at that point, I had given up writing (or, as I put it then, I was "taking a break"—a break that lasted well into my forties). I was in an acting class, and my friend and scene partner, Carol, and I couldn't find a scene for two women that hadn't been done to death. We had all watched the scenes between Portia and her lady-in-waiting, Nerissa, in *The Merchant of Venice,* and between Blanche and Stella in *A Streetcar Named Desire* so often we could recite the lines along with the actors. We were too old to play Juliet, Frankie in *The Member of the Wedding*, or a range of other classic characters. I had already worked on Beth Henley's *Crimes of the Heart* with another actress for this class, and Carol had done Wendy Wasserstein's *Uncommon Women and Others.* We were stumped. So on the night we had scheduled our first read-through, we instead split a bottle of wine and talked about how angry we were. There was a wealth of romantic scenes between a man and a woman, and the men in the class came in each week with interesting new scenes between two men—but we kept seeing the same two-woman scenes over and over, and half of them were "catfights"—violent or passive-aggressive confrontations, usually over a man, that struck us as unrealistic and insulting. Then we moved on to what we did want to see in a play, starting with friendship between women as a given.

Fueled by the wine and talk, I wrote a scene between two women, Peggy and Valerie—lifelong friends who get together to drink and reminisce after the funeral of Peggy's mother. As the scene progresses, their friendship is tested as they compare conflicting versions of old memories, and long-buried rivalries and hurts rise to the surface.

When we performed the scene in class and discussed its origin, other women in the class were enthusiastic and supportive. They encouraged me to expand it into a full play. One of the older women in the class commented that if we thought it was hard to find good parts now, just wait until we were fifty. So I added Peggy's mother's ghost as a sort of Greek chorus to the play's action. Eventually, as I kept working out the central conflict, I added two more characters, both women. In the final version, which I called *Fugue for Soprano Voices*, Peggy's teenage daughter adds sarcastic counterpoint to her mother's somewhat self-aggrandizing recollections, and the spirits of the two dead mothers provide commentary and correction to their daughters' childhood memories.

It was an interesting idea, though I didn't know enough about writing for the stage to bring it to full realization.

Looking at it now, from a distance of more than twenty-five years, I see glaring structural flaws and far more talk than action. On the other hand, it is remarkably free of clichés and pretentiousness. Perhaps because I was writing quickly and for an immediate, practical purpose—performing the scenes in class—I was able to escape the self-consciousness that usually plagued me. The characters speak in voices, and express emotions, that still ring true to me. In short, it was a creditable first effort.

About six weeks after I had completed the play, I was paging through *Backstage*, the actor's source for news about auditions and new productions, when an ad jumped out at me. A small but respected theater company in Manhattan's East Village was looking for one-act plays. I had not intended for this play to go further than my acting class, but on an impulse I sent it in. The next month, the managing director of the theater offered me a contract for a three-night run as part of a six-week one-act festival. She planned to pair it with another one-act with two male characters—a troubled pilot and the air traffic controller who talks him down. I was thrilled.

The thrill lasted from that moment through closing night. My play came to life in the hands of a gifted director working with intelligent, professional actors. A women's cable TV station filmed and broadcast a performance.

The other play offered an interesting contrast to mine, I

thought. It addressed the shifting power differential between the pilot and the air traffic controller, and the sometimes mixed motives that underlie surface altruism, intelligently and with dramatic flair. My friends and I agreed that the play lacked a certain emotional depth, but, like mine, it was a worthy attempt.

At the end of the last performance, the theater offered a question-and-answer session with the playwrights and directors. Audience members treated the other playwright with the respectful interest his play deserved. People asked about character motivation, about decisions of structure and dialogue, and about his research in aeronautics, and he answered them with intelligence and wit.

The questions directed at me were completely different. No one asked me about structure or dialogue. They didn't ask me about research, either. The audience seemed to take it for granted that I was writing about my own friends and family. (That was, indeed, the starting point, but the play took off from there.) Instead, what everyone wanted to know was: Why were there no men? Didn't I like men? Didn't I want to work with men? Hadn't we been able to find any male actors?

As Simone de Beauvoir said, "Man is defined as a human being, and woman as a female." No one commented on the absence of female characters in the other play. Presumably, the concern and curiosity about mine centered on the fact that there were no human beings in it. But that didn't occur to me then. Instead, I assumed that no one was asking me respectful technical questions because my play's structure was weak (it was) and the dialogue must be inferior, too (it wasn't). Obviously, the other play was a serious piece of work, and mine was defective and incomplete—and I must have been self-deluded to imagine they were comparable. Frankly, I can't remember my answers—only that I couldn't wait to get off the stage and crawl into a hole. And that's pretty much what I did—that was my last foray into creative writing for seventeen years.

How did I let this happen? It is easy to say, from this standpoint, that I "shouldn't" have let the prevailing mindset "get" to me. Of course I shouldn't have. (And truly, I didn't stop writing because of this one event—I had stopped writing a year or so earlier, and this was a last-ditch, nearly accidental effort to find my creative voice.) But producing and displaying art makes us vulnerable. Even if we believe we have achieved emotional distance from our material, we are still putting out our worldview for others to see and comment on. Maybe their responses and assumptions shouldn't matter—but they do, especially if they reinforce messages we've been hearing since childhood, and if we have been trained from birth to value others' opinions more highly than our own.

The story gets worse. When an audience member told me she was on the board of a repertory company in Brooklyn that she was sure would be interested in mounting a full production of my play, I took her number and promptly lost it.

I believe that I let the chance for a full-scale production slip away because I wasn't ready to face the conflict nearly every artist confronts sooner or later: Do we create work that expresses our authentic vision, or do we modify our vision to achieve greater acceptance and interest?

Like so many questions that apply to both genders, this one is particularly fraught for women. Of course, we all want to create art that reflects our deepest selves—otherwise, why go through all the work and angst involved? But art is also communication, and most of us cherish the hope of reaching others' minds and hearts with our words, our images, or our music. If we create art that no one wants to share, we feel alone with our vision, diminished and devalued. And if our experiences and ideas are considered inferior to begin with, the conflict between artistic expression and audience approval can feel overwhelming.

When I was writing my play, without any thought of a larger audience, the interest of my class nourished and inspired its development. Classmates offered criticism of the execution— certain lines and even entire scenes struck viewers as flat or confusing. Revising these parts didn't present a conflict because the goal was to clarify and refine my work to communicate my vision in a more accessible and interesting way.

But when the basic assumption underlying the play—that women lead rich, conflict-filled, interesting lives independent of men—was itself dismissed, the choices seemed to be to trash its moral and artistic core or to fight to justify it, accepting that it was probably doomed to be considered second-rate.

Again in hindsight, I can see that these probably weren't

the only choices. In fact, the questions that night probably didn't reflect the responses of the whole audience. If the woman from the Brooklyn theater group thought it deserved a full production, chances are she, and her company, would have supported an expanded all-woman play.

I think I couldn't see that because I was so isolated and vulnerable the night of the question-and-answer session. I was aware of sexism in the culture, but I hadn't fully explored the ways it had affected me or how susceptible I was to turning it against myself. It had been invigorating to work with the support of other women, but we were a class, not a support group—we didn't share experiences of dismissive treatment or brainstorm helpful responses and solutions. I didn't know that other women, many of whom are much more talented and accomplished than I am, go through similar ordeals every day.

Today, when my writing is dismissed as "women's work" (and it still does happen, unfortunately, though seldom in such an overt way), I'm able to keep my perspective. I realize that such comments reflect more about the limitations of the speaker than of my work. This is partly because I'm more experienced and mature, and partly because I'm more aware of the examples of successful contemporary writers, such as Eve Ensler and Caryl Churchill, whose work deals with "women's issues" in a brave and unapologetic way. Even more important, though, I am now blessed with a network of strong, enlightened women artists who support and sustain one another when our individual spirits flag.

When we don't have such a community to draw on, it is difficult to sustain our belief in the importance of our work. Elizabeth's experience of artistic isolation was much more profound than mine. She began writing her fiction at a time when women were discouraged from pursuing any kind of career, and it was a given that their art and ideas were frivolous and second-rate.

She told me, "I didn't come into my own as a writer until I started taking my own concerns seriously. First I tried to imitate the stories in girls' books and women's magazines. Then, when my teacher shamed me for my 'frivolity,' I took up 'men's themes'—war, death, alienation. But I wasn't experienced in those areas, at least not then, and I had no confidence or commitment. Even when I went back to writing 'women's stories' later in life, they were shallow, because I didn't believe I was writing about important issues. I thought I just wasn't good enough to write about the big themes, and that I'd made my peace with being a 'B' novelist. I had to realize that I was placing myself in that 'B' category—that I would, indeed, be a second-rate writer if I continued to denigrate the issues that were closest to my heart.

"There is great writing, and terrible writing, about every issue under the sun. I won't apologize for being fascinated by romance, friendship, and family issues. When animal behaviorists write about social and family organizations among chimps or wolves or what have you, that is serious and important—the day-to-day interactions, not just when the chimps lose it and kill each other or wander off from the pack for some guy adventures. Why on earth should writing about human relationships in the suburban United States be inherently less interesting?"

Of course writing about relationships is interesting and important when it's done well. Sometimes this is even recognized—usually when a man's name is attached to it. But many women writers who focus on relationships find themselves thrust into a "pink ghetto" regardless of the quality of their ideas or writing ability.

Like Elizabeth, novelist and memoirist Clea Simon deals with traditionally "feminine" subject matter. "I do feel like I've been ghettoized," she says, "first because I've written memoirs about family issues, and secondly because with my first two nonfiction books I really wanted to incorporate a larger worldview, others' experiences, and research. So, as one review stated, I wrote a 'self-help memoir.' Instead of being considered a serious writer, to some I'm simply an overemotive female, bleeding my sentimental family experience on the page. It's infuriating because it discredits the discipline of the writing, the research, the art, and the craft simply because the subject matter is seen as female. It's the same old prejudice, that I wrote about family instead of self, connection instead of aloofness, intimacy versus extroversion. I was seen as lesser, weaker."

Simon describes her third book, *The Feline Mystique: On the Mysterious Connection Between Women and Cats,* as "a kind of 'coming out.' It was my 'yes, I have feelings, yes, I love my pet, deal with it' book. I'm sick of being belittled and wanted to declare my style, my viewpoint, my mix of emotion and reason as points of pride."

Simon's subsequent books have been clever, erudite mysteries featuring a female investigative journalist and her cat. They are classified as "cozies"—a genre that lacks the cachet of the harder-edged police procedurals of equal or inferior quality and one that is associated with women writers and readers.

Simon refuses to buy into the myth of her second-rate status. "How do I navigate it? I feel rather defiant. I try to laugh at it. I know the quality of my work. I know what I'm striving for. If a certain literary clique wants to judge me by my subject matter rather than my actual writing, it's their loss."

Literary novelist Leora Skolkin-Smith also thinks her work, and that of several other female literary writers, has been underrated by the literary establishment because of traditionally feminine subject matter: "I feel that these days female writers of so-called 'serious literature' succeed only if they have chosen to write in male or malelike voices—strong voices which give examples of women capable of choice and triumph.

"Some of these books are wonderful. But they don't represent the full spectrum of women's lives and experiences, the lack of options and the insecurity and doubt many of us experience. Even Jane Austen's writing is denigrated as 'chick-lit' now. The thinking seems to be something along the lines of, 'Oh, these stupid women, all they think about is getting husbands; they're all so weak, blah, blah, blah; now we're all corporate and better than these ridiculous little girls.' It's chilling to really consider this."

Skolkin-Smith's perspective is that, although women have

made great strides in many areas, often the cost is continued devaluation of traditionally female pursuits. When a woman invades a domain that is considered "masculine," as Bonnie, the photographer, did, her inner struggle can become even more complex and fraught.

"I travel to war zones and to areas that are plagued by starvation and violence," Bonnie told me. "A real sense of camaraderie develops among journalists and photographers in these situations. Lots of times I'm the only woman at the hotel. Usually that's not an issue, but some of these guys tend to think it's a fraternity hazing, that a woman doesn't belong in a 'man's world,' and they need to put me in my place. They've run my bra up a flagpole, spied on me in the shower, and pinched my butt as I was focusing my lens. Once I found out about a plan to gang-rape me, just in time. What makes it worse is that it puts the other guys, the decent ones, in the position of 'defending' and 'protecting' me, and that alters the power balance even when we don't mean for it to. Suddenly I stand out; I'm 'the weaker sex,' I'm just different, and not as good, even to my friends.

"I love what I do, and I want to excel. If I show weakness, I might not get these assignments anymore. So I don't show it when I'm hurt, or even when I'm more frightened of my own coworkers than of the so-called enemy.

"Shutting down like that has a cost, personally and artistically. Just one example: I am more drawn, at least at times, to 'softer' pictures, even in war zones. I like to show the beauty of people: a child playing with a puppy, a mother nursing a baby, a kids' soccer team. Even in the midst of war and devastation, people find ways to love and to have fun. I think people need to know about that, to know that these people aren't another species just because they speak a different language or have darker skin—that they're just like us, they love their children, they are smart and silly and sad, they get married and they have birthday parties for their grandmothers and they cry when their children are hurt. And so it matters if they are killed or if they starve to death. It's important. This is important work.

"I don't think that's just a 'woman thing.' Several of my male colleagues go out of their way to find these pictures, too. But I find myself drawing back from them. I get into an angry mood and I don't want anyone to think I'm soft—and I don't want to be soft. It's not just about wanting to be seen as 'one of the guys' so I can do my work and keep getting the good assignments. It's deeper than that. I sometimes hate the part of me that's vulnerable, that reacts to the hazing by wanting to cry instead of just shrugging it off, or punching somebody, the way a macho guy would do. So I start hating anything that makes me feel—feel anything, really. I look at children playing and at first I want to smile, then I stomp on myself, and I think, *cheap sentimentality*. So for days all I'll shoot are straight news photos, accompaniments to articles, or the 'harder' photos, bodies ravaged by war or disease. Those are important parts of my work, of course, but when they are all I focus on I know I'm losing my balance. I get mean and cold, especially if there's another woman on-site who wants to befriend me. I can't stand to be associated with females. I'm lost."

Bonnie's "softer" pictures reflect at least as much strength and professionalism as the depictions of violence and degradation that are also part of her work. Male colleagues have been praised for their sensitivity in capturing these moments that are heartbreaking in their ordinariness. But Bonnie, like Elizabeth and Clea Simon, risks categorization of her work as "trivial" if she concentrates on more domestic scenes.

It is human nature to want to fit in with the dominant group. For our ancestors, the protection of tribal leaders could mean the difference between being warm and fed and being left out in the cold. For most of us in the 21st century, the situation isn't quite so dire, but we still desire group acceptance and approval, both for its material benefits and because we feel happier and more secure inside the circle. Often, we're willing to sacrifice a great deal—even the expression of our unique vision—to ensure the approval of our peers.

Again, every artist needs to accommodate the tension between artistic self-expression and producing work that will sell and be accepted. But when artists such as Bonnie feel they are penalized both for invading men's territory and for producing work traditionally associated with women, the result is frustration and despair. And because taking out our frustration on the dominant group would push us even further outside, too often we turn it against ourselves and other women.

Bonnie's "softer" side served as a shadow self in times of stress—and paradoxically, as is the case with shadow selves, her assumed toughness and "meanness" rendered her even more vulnerable by isolating her from other women who could help and support her. In therapy, she worked on validating and appreciating her "feminine" qualities of softness, compassion, and identification with other women. As she began reaching out to female colleagues, she learned that many of them struggle with similar issues. Several of them now participate in an informal support group that holds occasional face-to-face meetings and frequent group email exchanges. She told me recently, "We're not changing the world—at least, not yet. But we're giving each other the help we need to keep going in a tough field—and I'm learning to take pride in *all* the work I do. Anyone who thinks women are weak and silly hasn't met this group. I'm honored to be associated with them."

The "meanness" toward other women that Bonnie manifested at the beginning of therapy is not unique. Thriller writer and media expert M. J. Rose reports: "I've never experienced sexism within the thriller writing community. The publishers are more than willing to publish women, and the community is totally open and supportive to us. In fact, the male thriller writers are among the most inclusive group of writers I've ever met. My only issue is that reviewers favor men. But reviewers favor men in every genre.

"What I do have a problem with is female literary writers. More than 50 percent of the ones I've met have treated me like I write trash; they manage the worst faint praise and passive-aggressive comments of anyone I've ever dealt with in any business, bar none. From, 'Oh, for the kind of stuff you write, you do it well,' to 'I don't read those kinds of books,' to authors who ask me for favor after favor after favor and then tell me that 'I haven't ever tried to read one of your books; I only read literary fiction.'

"How that has affected me is to make me angry and keep me as far away from them all as I can get. How it has affected my creative output is not at all. This is too tough a gig to let them get me down."

Literary novelist Caroline Leavitt had a similar experience in the other direction: "I was friends with a very successful writer of smart romantic comedies. While I was struggling, in the midst of changing agents, she was super-supportive, telling me how good I was, how strong my work was, etcetera, etcetera. But I noticed that once I got a great literary agent, she began to make carping remarks, sniffing that 'adult drama' might be what critics wanted but a smart romantic comedy was more important. Worse, she gave interviews that mirrored conversations we had had—my bemoaning how hard it was to work some days, and her response that she would never put her characters through grief or pain because how could she ever do that to someone she loved? Since this was a writer who routinely got high six-figure advances and sold in the stratosphere, I couldn't understand her sniping at me or her sense of competitiveness. How could I possibly be a threat to her? The final incredible betrayal was her insistence that she read my new novel before my agent. Worried about my novel's merits, I refused until my agent read it and loved it, and then I sent it to her. Her response was cold and derogatory. She thought I should rewrite the whole book. It wasn't funny. It went on too long. She not only told me it was bad, but I began hearing stories through the literary network that she was bad-mouthing my work to others and that, in fact, she wouldn't blurb writers whose books I had blurbed."

These experiences reflect a fairly common phenomenon. When we feel threatened, often our response is to cover our vulnerability by turning "mean," to use Bonnie's word—and to direct our aggression not against those in power but against our peers. This is especially true if the peers seem to embrace qualities we feel despised or dismissed for, such as writing that does not conform to the prevailing idea of "importance," or if their work embodies ambitions, such as literary or artistic seriousness, that we may have worked to suppress in ourselves.

Filmmaker Terri Myers has also faced disparagement by those who would seem to be her natural allies: "Here's what happens when you are an artist and a woman, or an artist and a person of color, or, like me, both: Somebody will come along and tell you that you're not supposed to make certain things and that it's your responsibility to make other things.

"As a woman, I've been told that it was too bad I made a film about a man, that I should have made one about a woman instead. Who said this? A novelist who's a staunch feminist, someone who I thought should champion my right—my choice—to make anything I wanted. After all, I'm equal, right?

"As a person of color, I've been told that I shouldn't make work about subjects that aren't directly related to racial issues, because it's my responsibility to honor the struggle of my ancestors. Who told me this? A black filmmaker, someone who I thought would be happy that equal rights had reached such a milestone that any artist can make work about any subject in the world. What exactly did my grandparents fight for if it wasn't for my right to live and work as I choose, without suffering the same restrictions they did?

"I'm not letting white folks and men get out of jail free. There are plenty of uncomfortable complexities and wrong attitudes in the way they deal with someone like me. But it's most hurtful when the negative attitudes come from your own."

Myers's critically acclaimed documentary, *Not a Nickel's Worth of Doubt*, was produced in 1997. It was about her uncle, the artist Reginald Sanders, who recovered from a twenty-year creative block engendered by self-doubt to reinvent his career. "Racism contributed to those doubts, and I delved into that topic at appropriate points in the story, but that was only one part of it. There was no easy villain to blame. And, really, it was a film about art—the love of art and the fear of it—and that wasn't enough.

"Bucking the expectations, jumping hurdles that are set higher than they are for the majority, and fending off the scowls of my peers continue to be among my greatest difficulties in marketing myself as an artist.

"My strategy for ignoring this foolishness and continuing to make the work I want to make is simple: I have to. I'm wired to do this, and I'm tremendously unhappy if I'm not making something. I'm an artist and I'm no good at being anything else. Acceding to the mainstream's desire to dictate the content of my work isn't an option."

It is unusual for any woman to create art that's considered universal. As Myers's experience suggests, for a woman of color it is next to impossible.

Maria, the short story writer, has also found that others want to prescribe the subject matter of her work based on her gender and race. She told me, "A lot of my stories are set in the Bronx, in a neighborhood that's fictional but a lot like the one I grew up in. That causes problems for me, not with other writers, but in the community at large. If I write about people who have any kind of problems with drugs or alcohol, child abuse, unemployment, delinquency, I hear about it from my family, my neighbors, practically the entire Puerto Rican population of New York City. Everyone comes down on me for 'making us look bad.' It's worse, I think, because I'm a woman, so I'm supposed to write about nice things and be sensitive to everyone's feelings.

"White people write about these issues, and nobody thinks they're saying every white person in the world is a junkie or an abuser. Men even write memoirs about being junkies themselves, and everyone says how brave they are. But I'm supposed to airbrush everything I see, everything I write, to make a gritty *camino* in the Bronx look like Sesame Street. Or maybe they'd prefer that

I write only about rich white people. But guess what? Even if I could do that, even if I had the faintest interest in doing that, I could never get published, because they'd say, 'Who is she to be writing about us?' Basically, we can't win."

For some writers, publication itself is a galling reminder of second-rate status. Monica Jackson is a romance writer who is black. "I struggle with the same things all writers struggle with," she says. "It's a tough profession. Writing fiction requires self-exposure of the most intimate kind. We want to be read, to be exposed. It's an egocentric profession but also ego battering. When we define ourselves through our art, we open ourselves up to criticism and painful assaults. We open ourselves up to the possibility of being told we're no good, that we're less than others. For a black genre writer, this denigration is automatic, no matter how good our reviews.

"The majority of black genre fiction authors are marketed only to blacks, our books carried only in the stores that are located in areas with a significant black population. Our work is often shelved in the African American section rather than with the books of its genre unless we're one of the rare black best-sellers making the big lists.

"Most prefer to ignore the issue of race. But the anger erupts and leaks over into other aspects of your life. I know it's the reason black women can appear so angry and evil. You'd be too. We're treated like niggers. It's a hard word, but I use it because you asked about feelings, and that's how it feels."

Online reviews are a major source of publicity for romance novels. Jackson submitted her second novel to a well-known romance critic with a widely read blog. The reviewer, who acknowledged that this was the first "multicultural" romance she had read, disliked the book, which, Jackson says, "wasn't the bad part."

The "bad part" was that the book was reviewed differently from the way a novel featuring white characters would have been. "Her wording was that the characters appeared 'lily-white' and did things white people do," Jackson says.

"I was outraged that she expected a black *romance novel* to be some sort of ethnic learning experience for her. I was pissed that she held herself up as an expert on the romance genre while she'd never bothered to read a romance by a black person.

"I wrote her a private email about it that she promptly posted publicly. It caused a furor. The raw racism of the white romance readers was astonishing. It reflected what whites strive so hard to deny—that we haven't moved forward much since the mob in front of Little Rock High."

Meanwhile, other black romance writers contacted Jackson to tell her she shouldn't have expected fairness from the white community, that this treatment was par for the course. "My outrage turned to numbness," she says. "I shut down and I didn't write for months. I've never felt the same about the romance community since. The anger has never gone away.

"I thought writing fiction was the thing I wanted to do most in the entire world. That was before I realized that unless I was granted one of those rare tokens of being considered *universal*, and literary writers usually get all of those anyway, I'll always be considered a nigger, my writing fit only for niggers to read."

Jackson did go on to write again, though. Perhaps even more impressive, when the same critic blogged sensitively about the differential treatment of black victims of Hurricane Katrina, Jackson reached out to her, and they began a private dialogue about race and literature that they eventually moved into the public forum. They discovered some surprising areas of agreement and were able to learn from one another about the issues on which they disagreed. Last fall, Jackson took a chance and sent the critic her new novel, **Mr. Right Now**—which got a rave review.

It is difficult to consider and write about the ways women buy into assumptions about our own inferiority—and especially about the ways we turn our anger and frustration against ourselves, by shutting down or shutting up, and against one another, through disengagement and outright attacks. My grandmother used to warn me about "airing dirty laundry in public," and I must admit that I was tempted to tone down some of what was said here to present more of a united front. How much simpler and safer to write about beleaguered women artists pitted against the oppressive male establishment—to, in Maria's words, paint a gritty *camino* as Sesame Street. But we know that people, and art, are more complex and shaded than that—and as Jackson's experience shows, speaking out honestly can result in unexpected and rewarding alliances.

Finding and sustaining our unique voices amid the ghetto-ization, territorialism, and pressure, from without and within, to conform to a notion of "women artists" that may not fit our experience is a huge challenge. Some, such as Rose and Simon, are able to use opposition and denigration as fuel for their creative energy. Others, such as Bonnie and Skolkin-Smith, struggle to maintain the vulnerability that feeds their best work against a culture that punishes the appearance of weakness.

Often, when we feel that our work is unseen or misunderstood, we respond by shutting down. Either we become blocked, like Jackson, or, like Bonnie, we narrow our focus to "safe" subjects, those that may not express our full complexity or challenge our equilibrium. And too often, we turn on our fellow artists—particularly those who embody or represent the parts of ourselves that we are trying to suppress—demonizing or dismissing them as "the other." In doing so, we do a disservice, not only to them, but to ourselves.

I wish I had a solution to the broader issues raised here. Psychologists tend to deal in individual, not social, change—and social change is clearly what is called for.

Social change always starts with the individual, though, and one way to begin transforming the attitudes of the larger culture is to examine and address our own prejudices. The following exercise is designed to help you cross over into territory you may not have considered before.

Exercise:

stretching your sympathetic imagination

Consider a genre within your field that you have dismissed in the past. Seek out someone whose judgment you trust who is a fan of that genre. Ask her to recommend a work by a woman she believes you will like. Approach this work with as open a mind as you can muster. Be willing to be converted, as unlikely as that may seem. For example, I think of myself as primarily a "literary" writer and reader. I had never read a "chick lit" novel until a friend recommended *Bridget Jones's Diary*.

Write down your response to this work. Examine both your positive and negative reactions. Contemplate what these say about you and what you are trying to achieve in your own work. Are there any aspects of this genre you might like to incorporate into your work? What are they? What is stopping you?

One of the things I admired about **Bridget Jones's Diary** was Helen Fielding's openness about her character's weight obsession. The calorie counts and associated comments at the beginning of each "diary" entry were hilarious and also representative of contortions a lot of women go through but seldom talk about publicly. Later I drew on this example when writing a very different kind of story, in which a character obsesses about the way one of her toenails is starting to look like her mother's. The image was important to the story but I probably would have rejected it as trivial if I hadn't been so taken by Fielding's calorie counts and the realization that specific, idiosyncratic, "trivial" imagery can speak volumes and ground an abstract idea, such as "Bridget is neurotic about her weight" or "Amy worries about becoming her mother," in concrete reality. Now, when people denigrate "chick lit" books, I speak up with examples of books I've enjoyed and learned from. It's been a broadening experience for me, and I hope I'm helping, at least in a small way, to enhance respect for women working in other genres.

When Janna, the painter, tried this exercise, she decided to consult her sister. She told me, "Elaine is a great fan of what I've always called 'cute-crap art'—you know, Norman Rockwell, let's-make-everything-pretty paintings. She is nice about my work, but I know it disturbs her. I've always figured it was because of our horrendous childhood—she was running away from the truths I expressed in my art into this fake happy-dappy world, where all the adults are wise and loving and no one would ever, ever want to hurt a wittle girl or a puttytat. So I tolerated this in her, and basically, we never talked about it. We've been close in spite of this, but really, when you're talking about my life's work, that's a huge, gaping hole.

"She was surprised when I asked her to introduce me to some of 'her' art, and she was moved. I hadn't realized how much she felt I condescended to her about her taste. She brought me to a show of Grandma Moses paintings that was touring the country. She walked me through, talking to me about how happy it made her to see people celebrating, to see the beauty and symmetry of the landscape, the cozy interiors, and the sense of community. 'But it's fake,' I kept saying. 'It's a lie. Life isn't like that.'

"'It is, sometimes,' she said, 'just like it's violent and ugly sometimes, but that doesn't mean the whole world is garbage. Nobody paints things exactly the way they are. You have to focus on something and leave the rest out. I have enough ugliness in my life. I like to look at paintings that remind me of goodness.'

"I felt something open up in me. We were standing in front of a painting called A *Tramp at Christmas,* which shows a healthy, well-fed family inside a warm, comfortable house. A woman is putting food on the table; a little girl is playing with a kitten and a ball of yarn. The door is open, and a tramp is coming in from the outside. The family members are turning to look at him. Their faces and bodies are relaxed, welcoming. You know he's going to be invited in to share their bountiful meal.

"'I feel like that tramp,' I said to Elaine. I didn't expect her to understand what I meant—that I'm always on the outside, always the one tracking dirt into the house, the one who doesn't belong. But she did understand. She put her arm around me and said, 'Me, too. But here, I'm welcome.' We just stood there in the museum, holding one another and crying, until we realized how ridiculous we looked and started laughing.

"What part of Grandma Moses would I want to incorporate into my own work? That generosity, I guess. The ability to see a stranger, not as a threat, but as a welcome guest.

"I'm never going to make pretty art. I wouldn't want to, even if I could. There's more than enough of it, and not enough of us drawing attention to what people don't want to look at.

"I do think, though, that part of what I always thought was superior discrimination was really fear—ironically, exactly what I thought was going on with Elaine. I'm terrified of 'mushiness'—of drawing those cute kittens with hearts around their heads. The feeling is that if I were to give in to that naïveté, that hopefulness, I'd be fair game for someone else to come along and abuse me. I'd be that helpless child again.

"But maybe there is a place in my work for generosity, for hope—for love. I'm finding these qualities in my life more and more, as I open to them. Maybe I need to embrace them in my art as well. It's a lot to take in, a lot to consider—but I'm not ruling it out."

It is vitally important to an artist to keep stretching and growing throughout her lifetime. In the next chapter, we will explore ways to keep developing ourselves and our work into midlife and beyond.

the artists
we were
meant to be

growing

older

Chapter Eight

the year I turned thirty-five, I was working as a play therapist in a preschool for children with developmental disabilities while writing my master's thesis on the development of creativity in children with Down syndrome. The kids were adorable, but the work was unchallenging—I spent most of my days wiping noses, finger painting, and teaching basic life skills using dolls and toys. I had a secondary motive for being there, though: My husband and I thought it was time to get serious about starting a family.

One of the attractions of this job was the school schedule—nine to three, five days a week, with generous vacations, including three months off in the summer. After previous miscarriages, I had become pregnant in October, with a due date in early July. The preschool was housed in a large university that also offered a high-quality daycare center.

My life seemed to be in perfect order: I would graduate in the spring, give birth in the summer, get paid for staying home with the baby until the fall, and then return to work—on this abbreviated school schedule—knowing that my child was being well cared for a few doors down.

Then, during the winter, I miscarried again. I started to wonder whether my body was capable of carrying a baby to term. Even more discouraging, I was worn out from constantly attending to the needs of small children, and I was beginning to think I might be too old for new motherhood.

Without the prospect of a baby, the dead-end aspects of this job were too apparent. It was clear that if I wanted a fulfilling career as a therapist, I would have to return to school for my PhD. But the idea of going back to the classroom once more, as a middle-aged woman among newly minted college graduates, was daunting.

Right about this time, in 1987, I started reading about a group of young, hot writers whose cutting-edge books had taken the publishing world by storm during the past few years. Tama Janowitz, Bret Easton Ellis, Jay McInerney, and Mark Lindquist formed the core of this group, which also included Michael Chabon, Peter Farrelly, and Donna Tartt. Their work received admiring, even adulatory, reviews in literary publications, and their exploits—clubbing and partying with models and rock stars—were chronicled in newspapers and *People* magazine. These writers differed vastly in their backgrounds, style, and subject matter. The connecting threads among them were their iconoclasm and their youth: All had published their well-received first novels before the age of thirty. In fact, Bret Easton Ellis's **Less Than Zero** came out when he was nineteen. Suddenly youth and coolness were prerequisites for writers.

Despite some early luck publishing my stories and poems, I had not written anything substantial for seven or eight years. I had always assumed I would return to writing one day, though—that I would resolve the issues of inhibition and self-consciousness that had plagued me and silenced my authentic voice. I had thought there was time to work on these issues. Now it was clear that I had been a fool. I had dithered for too long, and now it was too late, for everything. I had missed the boat.

Of course, I did return to school, have a baby, and, eventually, start writing again. In all of these endeavors, though, I felt I was bucking the tide—that I was the lone bumbler among smart, together young people who had identified their goals early and pursued them with assurance and focus.

Culturally imposed expiration dates apply to a whole range of activities as we grow older, even as advances in medicine enable us to live longer, healthier lives, expanding the possibility of second and even third career choices and later-life parenthood. Despite the intelligence, creativity, and vigor of many older women in the public eye—and even their more positive and nuanced recent portrayals in the media—it's hard not to absorb the message that's also out there, that older women are pitiful or ridiculous. If you doubt this, just think of the phrase, "You _____ like an old lady!" Try to fill in the blank with a verb that would make this sentence a compliment.

Of course, "you write/paint/compose like an old lady" *should* be a compliment. Older women artists draw on a wealth of experience, wisdom, and practice that allows them to make invaluable contributions to any art. Even with the best possible image in mind of growing older, though, it's still hard to take up a deferred dream in middle age.

As long as we believe we'll write that novel, compose that concerto, or paint that masterpiece someday—and as long as "someday" remains a vague date in the future, after the loans are paid off, or the kids are grown, or we retire from our jobs—we can sustain the illusion that when we do get around to starting, our work will be brilliant, dazzling, and effortless, with no learning curve. Once we plunge in, we run smack up against our inexperience in solving technical and even conceptual problems, and we begin to suspect that our "brilliant" idea was the pipe dream of a self-deluded amateur. Feeling incompetent at something we care about is discouraging for anyone. When we compare our efforts to those of more accomplished artists half our age, though, the effect can be devastating.

Soon after I had started to write seriously again, I expressed doubt to my mentor, Michelle Herman, about whether it was too late for me to become a real writer—to surpass my "promising amateur" status and come into my own as an artist of power and substance. I didn't care about commercial success. I had another profession, one that I loved and that enabled me to support myself. But the idea of being a clumsy beginning writer at my age was galling to me, and I feared that that was what I would remain—that I had waited too long to get started, and now my ability to change, to accommodate new techniques and new perspectives, was compromised by my age. I dreaded being seen as foolish and pathetic for my efforts.

Michelle responded to my expression of self-doubt by

sending me a copy of Tillie Olsen's *Tell Me a Riddle*. This exquisite collection of stories was published when Olsen was forty-eight years old. She had started a novel at nineteen but abandoned it to raise four children, and she didn't take up writing again until her youngest child started school, when Olsen was forty. The stories are notable for their depth and wisdom, which Olsen had clearly been developing all those years when she wasn't writing. Her even wiser book of essays, *Silences*, appeared in 1978, when Olsen was sixty-six.

As I stumbled through my first serious stories, struggling to capture my vision in words, writing dialogue that sounded stilted and descriptions that kept coming out as clichés, feeling clumsy and hopeless, Olsen's example kept my fingers from the "delete file" button. I told myself repeatedly that, like her, I had been learning and growing all the time I wasn't writing, and the wisdom I had gleaned from all of my experiences would find expression if I just persevered through the learning stage.

I did persevere, and while I'm hardly at Olsen's level, I have written stories I am proud of and that have been published and praised by others. But what I didn't know then, and wish I had, is that it's all a "learning stage." The risk of appearing foolish—of taking a glaringly wrong turn, of falling flat, of exposing our ignorance or limitations—is an integral, inescapable part of creative production. The willingness to take on this risk—to shape and express our inner vision, to forge on despite anxiety about how it will be received—is what separates the true artist from the hack, regardless of the success or failure of any particular endeavor.

Knowing this enables me to push through when I despair of ever being able to get a story right. I used to imagine that there were secrets to good writing—that "literature" was a foreign country whose terrain "real" writers were familiar and comfortable with, and I didn't even have a map. It's clear to me now, though, that there is no map—each new work is an unexplored continent, and it's up to us to chart the territory. The knowledge that it's always going to be this way—that there are no shortcuts, the roads are never paved, and the journey is not going to become easy or predictable over time—can be frightening, but it's also exhilarating.

Of course some aspects of creativity do get easier. We master technique through practice, and I, at least, have a lot of practice to catch up on. The process of laying out a story, figuring out the central conflict, and identifying the images that will (and won't) deepen the story's meaning while moving the narrative forward becomes a bit more familiar each time. Even living through the insecurity of that "lost" feeling over and over has helped me to stay the course—I just remind myself that I've felt this way before and come out on the other side; chances are I can do it again. Maybe if I'd stuck with my writing all those years I would have perfect verbal facility by now, and I would be completely comfortable traveling blind. Maybe. In the end, though, every creative person, young or old, must approach each new work as a beginner.

Despite the knowledge that we grow wiser every year, many artists do worry about the effect of aging on their work. Both "old beginners" and professionals who have been practicing their art for many years express concerns about forgetfulness, fuzzy thinking, and reduced energy and stamina. These are valid concerns, up to a point.

One area in which aging has a definite impact is in memory retrieval. Most people have had the experience of "blanking out" on a friend's name, the punch line of a joke, or the name of an actor. Statistically, this happens more frequently as we age, and it can be frustrating to think of the perfect line of dialogue or musical transition on the elevator, only to lose it by the time we get home. When I was in my twenties, I could compose ten-page speeches while washing the dishes. Now I keep a notebook and pen handy all the time. I've learned from experience to write down even those ideas that seem so important there is no way I could forget them. Lisette, the composer, sings softly into a small recording device that she carries everywhere.

The fatigue factor is real, too. For most of us, time seems to speed up as we age, and suddenly there aren't enough hours in the day. Nearly every important undertaking takes longer, and saps more of our strength, at fifty than it did at twenty. We may find that we need to be ruthless in trimming nonessential activities from our schedules. Elizabeth, the eighty-two-year-old novelist, told me, "The most important word I learned after fifty was 'no.' I used to be so grateful for invitations to speak to book groups or read my work that I'd exhaust myself traveling from one site to another. I love my readers, but I ended up too busy and tired to write. I've had to be more selective as my energy declines. I've also learned to say no to social engagements that don't nourish me. I make time for my children and grandchildren and a few close friends—beyond that, I need to protect my writing time."

Another ability that declines with age is divergent thinking, popularly known as the ability to "think outside the box," to create new forms and innovative means of expression. The iconoclasts and innovators in any field are often—though not always—young people. Many breakthroughs in mathematics and science are achieved by younger practitioners, who may then spend their later careers refining and expanding on their early work.

Young artists create new forms—experimental plays, conceptual art, cutting-edge music—that often shock older audiences and offend the establishment. Frequently, through the years, the new form becomes more familiar and accepted, and eventually it is folded into the established canon.

Janna, the painter, began creating her strange, disturbing portrayals of frightened and vulnerable young girls when she was in high school. Her work was met with outrage, and even now, in New York, parent and teacher groups sometimes stage protests of her showings and circulate petitions to have her work banned. "It's not a matter of trying to be controversial," she told me. "I paint what is inside me, in the way that best expresses my vision.

It just doesn't happen to fit in with a particular tradition or convention, and so I think it confuses people."

The capacity for divergent thinking is thought to peak in the twenties. However, cognitive scientists are quick to point out that these are statistical trends, and that differences between individuals are more marked and significant than differences between age groups. It's also not clear whether the cause is an organic process or simply the accumulation of experience guiding us to repeat what has worked in the past.

Janna is twenty-six now. It will be interesting to see how her style evolves through the years. Her comment after completing the exercise on exploring other genres—that she wanted to incorporate Grandma Moses's "generosity" into her work—interested me in this regard.

Lisette, the composer, also produced work in her youth that was considered "cutting edge." She feels lucky that the first person who heard it was Christine, her mentor, because "she was open to the unfamiliar. A more conservative teacher might have responded the way I do now when the kids in my classes try to get me interested in 'metal' or hip-hop—with a blank stare and the comment, '*This* is supposed to be *music*?' I try to be as open to their innovations as Christine was to mine, but it's hard, the way it's hard to learn a foreign language after a certain age."

Lisette's childhood was steeped in the musical tradition of her church, but she consciously rejected its influence on her compositions. "I needed to go off in my own direction," she said. "Music was my private rebellion, my escape from the stifling expectations of my family and community. I dreamed of living in pure sound, and that's what I tried to capture in my compositions. I experienced any suggestion to incorporate African American themes into my work as coercion, as pressure to function as a representative of my race rather than as a true, independent artist.

"Over the past few years, though, 'pure sound,' unconnected to other human beings, has started to feel like a lonely endeavor."

After Lisette "visited" with Harriet Tubman in the role model exercise, she found herself humming traditional African American tunes, especially "Follow the Drinking Gourd," the song that transmitted coded information about the Underground Railroad to escaping slaves.

"I had never used a recognizable melody in my work before, but I was haunted by these songs. I'd grown up hearing and singing them. I've started weaving them into a composition as a way of communicating with those anonymous composers who came before me, of thanking them, and of thanking Harriet Tubman, too, for her strength and bravery."

As Lisette's artistic evolution shows, declines in divergent thinking are often balanced by an increased capacity for convergent thinking (again, statistically speaking). This is the ability to draw connections and identify similarities among events, ideas, and phenomena and to locate them within a contextual framework. In other words, a painter might be more aware of the formal relationships among objects or the historical underpinnings of her work. A composer may respond to a unifying theme in seemingly disparate musical sequences— and, like Lisette, seek to weave these into a cohesive whole. As a writer, I find myself drawn, more and more, to examining historical parallels—between the Vietnam War and the current conflict in Iraq, between my son's childhood and mine—and exploring how they compare to other wars, other childhoods— in other words, to discovering what may be universal aspects of childhood and war.

I think there is a humility that can accompany increasing age, a sense that our work constitutes one thread in a vast tapestry. When we are younger, we tend to think of ourselves as the center of the universe. We find it hard to believe that anyone else has loved with the passion we feel for our first crush, or that our elders were ever as intelligent, idealistic, or creative as we are. We imagine that all truly interesting ideas originated with us, or, at least, with our generation. With age comes a sense of proportion that allows us to integrate what we see, hear, and think in a new way. Rather than inventing new forms and introducing new ideas, we are more likely to reexamine and illuminate what we already know. And that is an invaluable gift.

When my clients lose sight of the advantages of growing older, I remind them of the many gifted, courageous women who have developed their unique vision through middle age and beyond. Here is a partial list:

- Mary Aline Mynors Farmar (Mary Wesley) published her first novel, *Jumping the Queue,* at seventy. She went on to write nine more best-selling novels, including *The Camomile Lawn,* which was made into an award-winning British TV series.

- Georgia O'Keeffe continued painting and drawing into her nineties, despite increasing vision problems due to macular degeneration.

- Martha Graham danced until age seventy-six, when she "retired" to choreograph well into her nineties.

- Anna Mary Robertson (Grandma Moses) began painting in her seventies and sold her first painting at age seventy-eight. At age one hundred, she completed a series of illustrations of Clement C. Moore's *A Visit from St. Nicholas* ("'Twas the Night Before Christmas"); the edition remains popular today.

- Laura Ingalls Wilder was in her fifties and sixties when she wrote her "Little House" books.

- Joan Tower, the first woman to win the Grawemeyer Award in Music Composition, continues to produce exciting and innovative music at age sixty-eight, with no sign of slowing down.

- Alice Munro's latest (and, she says, her last, though I hope not) story collection, *The View from Castle Rock,* was published in 2006. Many critics agree that it contains some of her finest work. She is seventy-five.

- Grace Paley continues to write stories and poems of breathtaking beauty and simplicity that challenge prevailing political and social assumptions. She is eighty-four.

Elizabeth, the novelist, is also a source of inspiration. "I'm a much better writer now than I was in my twenties," she told me. "My writing improved during the years I thought I'd given it up. I was accumulating experience, reading widely, and discovering what I really felt and believed by rubbing up against people whose beliefs challenged mine. Would I have been a better writer if I'd written ten pages a day all those years? There's no way to know. It's also possible, though, that the experience of living my life directly, without continually documenting my thoughts as I do now, nourished another part of me that feeds into my work."

Elizabeth, at eighty-two, is realistic about the limitations imposed by age: "I don't think or type as quickly, I forget half of my brilliant ideas before I write them down, and I fall asleep watching the evening news." There are advantages, too, though: "My children, and even my grandchildren, are grown now. I'm not responsible for anyone but myself. So I follow my own inclinations. If I'm immersed in working out a tough plot issue at dinnertime, I don't have to interrupt my work to cook or even to eat—I just snack on fruit and crackers and keep plowing through. If I wake up in the middle of the night with an idea or a line of dialogue in my head, I just get up and write. I don't worry about waking anyone else or being too tired for the carpool or PTA meeting the next day. I think my books are more cohesive now that my time isn't chopped up. I have a sense of uninterrupted flow that wasn't there when I was younger."

The control Elizabeth now enjoys in setting her own schedule, pruning her social life, and working according to internal prompts is reflected in a new artistic freedom: "Quite frankly, I don't give a hoot what anyone thinks—not my neighbors, the critics, even my publisher. Life is too short to spend it worrying about other people's expectations. I'm grateful for my readers, but nowadays I'm more interested in writing what I want to write, in exploring the themes that interest me, than in being read."

Elizabeth is the oldest artist I have worked with, but other artists have also expressed a developing sense of freedom and independence as they age. As more artists remain healthy and productive into old age, it will be interesting to see whether another trend develops beyond the divergent/convergent shift— perhaps a synthesis of the two ways of seeing and thinking that combines an appreciation of tradition and connection with the independence and fearlessness that come from a lifetime of meeting challenges and surmounting obstacles.

As we have explored in this book, aspiring artists confront numerous obstacles to full artistic expression. Our families, communities, and the culture at large may discourage us from pursuing our dreams, especially when we're not aware of, or acquainted with, successful women in our field. We may internalize these negative attitudes, allowing self-doubt to hold us back. Even when we do create art, the message that our self-worth depends on being attractive and pleasing others can hinder us from acknowledging and expressing the deep and important truths embodied in our shadow selves. And many women's careers are sidetracked by family obligations that sap time and energy, even as they nourish our souls and expand our imaginations.

Put simply, most of us need to work harder to achieve our dreams than men do. For this reason, we often don't come into our own as artists until later in life. We may feel this puts us at a disadvantage, and even, as I did, that we have "missed the boat."

Nothing could be further from the truth. Each of us is her own boat, and we sail when we're ready, at our own pace. We are not in a race against other artists—we can't be, because there isn't a finish line. We improve with practice, and we can certainly learn from more accomplished artists, but comparing our work to anyone else's—or even to an idea of what we might have produced if our lives had been different—is not only unproductive, it runs counter to the nature of artistic creation. The task of every artist, at every stage, is to express and refine our unique vision to the best of our ability, using every resource available to us. No one else has had our experiences; no one else sees the world the way we do—so there is no basis for comparison and no timeline—just a continuing adventure, often fraught with danger and frustration, but studded with unexpected beauty, discovery, and richness.

Exercise:

extending your artistic autobiography

Take some time to reread your recorded responses to all of the exercises in this book. Think about how every event, every interaction you have recorded has helped to shape the artist you are today. Consider the positive influences of mentors, supportive friends and family members, and role models, but don't neglect the bad experiences—the rejections, discouraging messages, or even abuse—because these have also helped to shape your personal vision in important ways. If it were in your power to alter your artistic journey in any way you wanted to, what would you change? Is there a way to make these changes, starting now?

Imagine yourself in ten years. Draw a picture of this person, surrounded by her work. As always, don't worry about the quality of the drawing; just try to translate the scene from your imagination to the page in as much detail as possible. What do you think your art will be like ten years from now? Is this a direction you want to go in?

Look at the picture of your older self. Talk to her as though she were a real person. Tell her about your hopes and fears for the future. Imagine that she is responding. What does she say?

When Maria did the life review part of this exercise, she again expressed gratitude for her teacher and mentor, Mrs. Núñez; for the happy accident of finding a first-rate creative writing program at the college she attended; and for her husband and daughter, who, she said, "teach me every day about love—and love is the most creative force I can imagine." We discussed her family's strictness and lack of understanding in the light of their influence on her artistic development. She said, "I would probably have trusted myself more if they had encouraged me, if they could have seen me as a person with gifts and strengths of my own instead of just as a less competent version of my sister. On the other hand, the person who tried hardest to beat me into conformity—my grandmother—is also a great source of inspiration to me. All of her harshness came from her own fear of not fitting into this scary new country. When I'm writing I think about how she was uprooted here, from a farm to a big city where she didn't even understand the language, and I realize how easy my life is in comparison. Rejection slips and bad reviews don't seem nearly so intimidating in that light. Besides, I often use an *abuelita* character in my stories to illustrate the magic and the craziness of the old ways. So she was helping me become a writer even when she tried her best to stifle me."

When I asked her what she would change, she responded, "My wimpiness. I let myself be controlled and intimidated by my family's disapproval. I'm better than I used to be at believing in myself, making time to write, and promoting my work, but I have so far to go, and I lost so much time. I wish I had been more selfish and self-directed in going after what I want and need."

I asked whether she could imagine making these changes now. Her eyes filled. "I've made so many changes this year, but I can feel myself slowing down. I'm working better now that I have more time to myself, but I'm still the one Melissa wakes up at night when she needs something, I'm still in charge of arranging her playdates and her pediatrician visits, I'm still the one who puts my own work on hold if she's sick or upset. I wouldn't want it any other way, but I'm not a teenager anymore, and my energy is limited. This week she had a bad ear infection, and neither of us slept for days. I'd started work on a story, but now I can't even remember where I wanted to go with it. I wish I'd been bolder when I was growing up, so I'd be established now, but I don't see making any radical changes at this point. It just isn't a good time to work on selfishness."

I asked her to draw herself in ten years. She drew a picture of herself sitting at her computer. Maria is talented at drawing, and the picture was a good likeness. She added lines around her eyes and mouth. "I made my hips smaller, because I hope I'll have lost the baby weight by then," she commented.

"What about your work? What will that look like?"

She hesitated and then admitted, "I'm drawing a blank." She added dark circles under her avatar's eyes. "All I can think of is sleep. In ten years maybe I'll have an uninterrupted night's sleep."

"How old will Melissa be in ten years?"

Maria's eyes widened. "Oh, my God—she'll be eleven! She'll be in school all day. Even in five years, she'll start going to bed by herself, feeding and dressing herself, and reading and making friends." Just realizing that she would eventually have more control over her life gave Maria new energy.

"What will your work look like then?" I repeated.

She picked up a brown pencil and began blocking in a row of buildings behind the image of herself. "There's a set of stories I've been thinking of, about people who live on a certain street in the Bronx. Each story has a different protagonist, but they all know each other and show up in one another's stories. Some are related—a thirty-five-year-old woman gets divorced and comes back home to raise her children near her *abuelita*; meanwhile, a father gets Alzheimer's and goes to live with his son's family. Some have been neighbors for years; some are white people moving in and gentrifying the neighborhood."

As she spoke, Maria began drawing the characters in, and the page came alive. Men in undershirts sat on stoops drinking beer; a worker painted a house while a well-dressed white couple looked on; and an old man ran naked down the street, chased by a distraught-looking young woman holding a baby. "That's the Alzheimer's grandpa," she told me, growing increasingly excited. "Here's the daughter-in-law. Her husband just dumps the grandpa on her and goes off every day to his big-deal job. She's only twenty-three, and she's got a baby and now this crazy demented old man to look after, and she thinks her life is over."

Recalling the technique of Mrs. Núñez, Maria's grammar school mentor, I asked, "And what happens then?"

"He saves her! He frees her, see? He's not embarrassed to run around naked or to pee out the window. She stops being so self-conscious about not looking like a model—she realizes she doesn't have to be perfect, either. He says whatever comes into his head. He calls his son a poopyface bastard, and she sees that's exactly what he is. So she stops worrying about not knowing what to say to people and starts saying what she thinks. In the end, she and the baby and the grandpa move into their own apartment, and she falls in love with his new home health aide."

"What a wonderful story," I commented. "And that's exactly the boldness you want for yourself, right?"

"Right." Maria began coloring in her own picture again, widening her hips. "This is probably more realistic. In ten years, I'll be too busy writing to worry about looking like a model."

She hesitated. "This exercise is supposed to help you plan for the future, not write a story in the present, isn't it?"

I was afraid for a moment that she was going to fall into her old trap of doubting herself, of apologizing for her originality in not coloring within the lines. Instead, she grinned. "This is my plan, see? That old man is who I want to be—not crazy and demented, but free to express myself, not so scared of what everyone thinks. And how will I get there in ten years if I don't start now?"

for further reading

Apostolos-Cappadona, Diane, and Lucinda Ebersole, eds. *Women, Creativity, and the Arts: Critical and Autobiographical Perspectives*. New York: Continuum, 1995.

Arnold, Karen D., Kathleen Diane Noble, and Rena Faye Subotnik. *Remarkable Women: Perspectives on Female Talent Development*. Cresskill, NJ: Hampton Press, 1995.

Bepko, Claudia, and Jo-Ann Krestan. *Singing at the Top of Our Lungs: Women, Love, and Creativity*. New York: HarperCollins, 1993.

Bergmann, Maria V. *What I Heard in the Silence: Role Reversal, Trauma, and Creativity in the Lives of Women*. Madison, CT: International Universities Press, 2000.

Brandeis, Gayle. *Fruitflesh: Seeds of Inspiration for Women Who Write*. San Francisco: HarperSanFrancisco, 2004.

Cameron, Julia. *The Artist's Way: A Spiritual Path to Higher Creativity*. New York: Jeremy P. Tarcher/Putnam, 2002.

Ealy, C. Diane, PhD. *The Woman's Book of Creativity*. Berkeley: Celestial Arts, 2000.

Firestone, Linda A., PhD. *Awakening Minerva: The Power of Creativity in Women's Lives*. New York: Warner Books, 1997.

Flaherty, Alice W. *The Midnight Disease: The Drive to Write, Writer's Block, and the Creative Brain*. Boston: Houghton Mifflin, 2004.

Guerrilla Girls. *The Guerrilla Girls' Bedside Companion to the History of Western Art*. New York: Penguin, 1998.

Heilbrun, Carolyn. *Writing a Woman's Life*. New York: Ballantine Books, 1988.

Johnson, Sarah Anne, ed. *Conversations with American Women Writers*. Lebanon, NH: University Press of New England, 2004.

Kallet, Marilyn, and Judith Ortiz Cofer, eds. *Sleeping with One Eye Open: Women Writers and the Art of Survival.* Athens, GA: University of Georgia Press, 1999.

Kavaler-Adler, Susan. *The Compulsion to Create: Women Writers and Their Demon Lovers.* New York: Other Press, 2000.

McMeekin, Gail. *The Twelve Secrets of Highly Creative Women: A Portable Mentor.* Berkeley: Conari Press, 2000.

Rosenman, Ellen Bayuk. *A Room of One's Own: Women Writers and the Politics of Creativity.* Farmington Hills, MI: Twayne, 1994.

Turner, Joan, and Carol Rose, eds. *Spider Women: A Tapestry of Creativity and Healing.* Winnipeg, MB: J. Gordon Shillingford, 1999.

acknowledgments

acknowledgments pages frequently list people "without whom this book would never have been written." Until last year, I assumed that was hyperbole. But this book *really* would never have been written without my Seal Press editor, Jill Rothenberg, and two of my favorite writers, Andrea Buchanan and M. J. Rose, because I would never have thought of it on my own.

M. J., a best-selling novelist, is the proprietor of **Buzz, Balls & Hype**, a widely read blog about the book publishing industry. She and I became friends while collaborating on a proposal for a book on procrastination in novel writing. In 2005, she launched a marketing company, AuthorBuzz.com, which encroached on her blogging time, and she sought a guest blogger to share some of the writing. M. J. knew that most of my therapy clients were creative artists, and she suggested that I contribute a weekly advice column for writers. The column, "The Doctor Is In," made its debut in October 2005.

That's where Andi came in. She quoted one of my columns in her *Mother Shock* blog. I had contributed an essay to Andi's recently published anthology, *It's a Boy: Women Writers on Raising Sons*. Jill, Andi's editor at Seal, saw the quote, followed the link to my column, and emailed Andi asking whether she thought I might be interested in writing a book on women and creativity—and we were off.

From the original book proposal through final edits, this triumvirate coached me through the process of conceiving, writing, and publishing a book. No amount of money could have bought the education I got, and my gratitude is beyond words.

My agent, Deborah Grosvenor, shared her considerable wisdom and expertise freely and always to my advantage.

My husband, Bill Donnenberg, read each chapter in its raw form, before I dared to show it to anyone else. He gave me thoughtful, incisive feedback that never once included the terms "shrill," "doctrinaire," or any of the other adjectives women tend to hear when we talk openly about the elephant in the room.

Kate Maloy and Lisa Peet read early (post-Bill) drafts of problematic chapters and offered invaluable comments and suggestions.

Parts of this book were completed at a time of intense stress and worry for our family. My brother, Jack O'Doherty, and my sister-in-law, Vivian Cruz-O'Doherty, pulled more than their weight to allow me to meet deadlines. I am also blessed with a circle of writer friends who truly understand how hard it is to balance the requirements of the work we are called to do against the crises of the people we love. I was overwhelmed with offers of food, drink, childcare, massage, transportation, and "anything—just call." If I thanked everyone who deserved it, there would be no room in this book for the actual text. I am grateful to all, but especially to Masha Hamilton and Caroline Leavitt.

Finally, and most important, I'm deeply indebted to the clients, workshop participants, friends, and acquaintances whose stories appear in these pages and whose experiences have informed my thinking and shaped my technique. Artists are wonderful people to work with and write about, and I feel privileged to do the work I do.

about
the
author

d r. Susan O'Doherty is a clinical psychologist in private practice who specializes in helping clients to discover and develop their creative gifts. She is also an advice columnist whose weekly online column, "The Doctor Is In," helps writers break through their barriers to creativity. Her essays have appeared in several anthologies, including It's a Boy: Women Writers on Raising Sons and About What Was Lost: Twenty Writers on Miscarriage, Healing, and Hope, and her stories and poems have been published in Northwest Review, Apalachee Review, Eureka Literary Magazine, and Literary Mama. She lives in Brooklyn with her husband and son.